AMAZON REVIEWS

★★★★★ **Secret to success — Consulting Case Interviews.** In graduate school I browsed many books on consulting case interview preparation. This was the only book I read. The clear, consistent way of thinking through how to manage case interviews made sense. Rather than focusing on formulas, frameworks (e.g., Porters Five Forces), or just examples, Cosentino classifies cases into sensible categories and coaches the student through how to think about answering. Additionally, he gives valuable tips on how to get comfortable in the interview.

The true proof however was that I interviewed with the two top strategy consulting firms and received offers from both. I would highly recommend this book to anyone considering interviewing with top strategy consulting firms.

★★★★★ **Outstanding prep for case interviews,** *Case in Point* is in my view the best book of its type on the market. The top firms vary their cases from interviewer to interviewer — Cosentino's book provides a good system for tackling any case that you're presented. This book got me extremely well-prepared for my interviews. I just received a summer associate offer from what's arguably the top consulting firm, despite my non-business background.

★★★★★ **This is excellent.** This is probably the best consulting book on the market for undergrads looking to get a job in a top consulting firm after college. I own the Vault Guide to the Case Interview and felt this was MUCH better because it gives you a system to follow, not just a bunch of random structures and cases. Cosentino does a great job of putting all these pieces together in a very useful book.

★★★★★ **Great book for consulting preparation.** Cosentino's compilation of cases is a superb way to prepare for management consulting case interviews. Not only does he provide a wide variety of cases (from market sizing to acquisition opportunity to dipping profits) he also offers several helpful frameworks for approaching consulting cases in general. I would highly recommend this book to anyone planning to do consulting interviews (and they're tough!).

★★★★★ **Having a job interview? Use this book: it's a must.** I used this book as a tool to prepare for interviews; and it really helped me. In this tough period, I followed the Ivy Case Method proposed, and it didn't fail. The book presents in a very readable way what to expect in an interview and how to create your best strategy. I'm usually very skeptical about these kinds of books, but I must say that Cosentino is able to attract the reader and through anecdotes and concrete examples, to keep the reader's interest till the last page. Definitely a must.

★★★★★ **Got me a consulting job!,** I was VERY nervous about getting a good job after school. I compared several interview guides and found some to be incomplete and others to be too long & confusing. Cosentino's *Case in Point* was easier to understand and covered the key techniques/frameworks behind case interviews. I practiced the sample cases and I eventually got a job in strategy consulting.

also by Marc P. Cosentino

The Harvard College Guide to Consulting Case Questions

The Harvard College Guide to Consulting

The Harvard College Guide to Investment Banking

Case In Point

Complete Case Interview Preparation

THIRD EDITION

Marc P. Cosentino

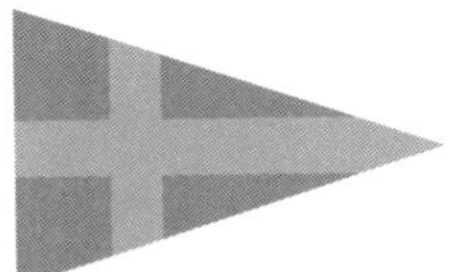

Published by Burgee Press, Needham, MA

Acknowledgments

Thanks are owed to all the students from around the world who contributed thoughts and case questions.

Burgee Press
P.O. Box 920654
Needham, MA 02492

As with all case questions, we assume facts not in evidence, as well as generous assumptions. Familiar companies are used as examples because of the power of their brand and their familiarity to the general public. Information concerning the actual companies cited as examples may not be accurate. This information was based on research, but should not be used as reliable, up-to-date data.

Edited by Tara Zend and Leisa Cosentino

ISBN 0-9710158-0-5
Library of Congress Cataloging-in-Publication Data:
Case in Point: Complete Case Interview Preparation / Marc Cosentino — 3rd ed.
Library of Congress Card Number 2001117521

First Printing, 1999
Printed in the United States of America

Second Edition 2001
Third Edition 2004

Contents

For Leisa, Emily and Colin

The mind is wondrous. It starts working from the second you're born and doesn't stop until you get a case question.

1 : Introduction

Our client is Anheuser-Busch. Their flagship product is Budweiser. They want to know if they should switch Budweiser from glass to plastic bottles. What are the advantages and disadvantages of such a move? And estimate for me the size of the U.S. beer market.

Consulting firms are in the business of renting out brains. Consultants get paid to synthesize massive quantities of foreign data, toss out the irrelevant information, structure an approach to a given client issue, and hypothesize logically and creatively before people of power and influence (like bigwigs at Anheuser-Busch). That's why consulting firms put so much weight on the case question– because it allows them to judge how logically and persuasively a potential consultant (i.e., you) can present a case. In essence, a case interview is a role-playing exercise.

In order to nail a case interview, you need to know both how to prepare and how to perform. This book will help you do both. It walks you through the overall consulting interview, teaches you how to conduct your research, tells you what the consulting firms are looking for in a candidate, explores the various types of case questions, and then introduces you to the Ivy Case System©.

As a career officer at Harvard for over fifteen years, I've helped more than seven thousand of the nation's top students prepare for consulting interviews. During this time, students have tirelessly memorized individual frameworks and then have struggled to decide which one(s) to apply. All the while, the case questions given by consulting firms have become increasingly complex. The standard frameworks of the past, while still valuable, aren't enough to solve these sophisticated cases. I've developed The Ivy Case System in order to simplify things. This system will allow you to make an impressive start (without a long and awkward pause) and ensure that you approach the answer in an organized and logical way. The difference between a framework and a system is that a framework is a tool; a system is a process with all the tools built in. The Ivy Case System is the most sensible and comprehensive case interview strategy you can learn.

Keep in mind that case questions help educate you during your job search by acting as a self-imposed screening device. Is this the type of work you want to be doing? Is this the type of environment in which you can learn and flourish? You need to ask yourself, "Do I enjoy problem solving? Do I enjoy these types of questions and issues?" Case questions can and should be fun.

The best way to prepare is to hunker down and (i) read this book and don't skip any pages; (ii) attend all case question workshops sponsored by consulting firms or your Office of Career Services; (iii) practice with your econ professor, roommates, friends, and anyone you know who worked or is currently working in consulting (see The Roommate's Guide, page 162); and (iv) read this book again and don't skip any pages.

Sounds like you better start reading...

Relax, it's worse than you think. If you figure the odds of getting chosen for an interview, having all the interviewers like you, and making it through seven to 10 cases, you'll be spending next semester's tuition on lottery tickets. But you know what? You faced much greater odds when you applied to a top school. Not only were you accepted, you've thrived. So forget about the odds and concentrate on you. If there were ever a time for tunnel vision, this is it. Besides, the recruiters don't know about the time you... well, they don't know and we're certainly not going to tell them. You head into an interview with a clean slate.

INTERVIEW (time : what firms look for)

- **Intro**
  quick exchange : overall package, eye contact, smile
- **Questions About You**
  5-10 min : leadership, drive, enthusiasm
- **Why Consulting?**
  2 min : commitment to consulting
- **Possible Math Question**
  1 min : grace under pressure
- **Case Question(s)**
  10-15 min : poise, analytical & communication skills
- **Your Questions**
  3 min : intelligence, homework
- **The Grand Finale**
  2 min : selling—why hire you?

This chapter will walk you through a first-round interview and will show you how to prepare properly for each step. Some firms set up two back- to-back 30-minute interviews for the first round. In these interviews, one interviewer spends more time questioning you about yourself and then gives a shorter case question, while the other interviewer spends less time on you and more time on the case.

✣ Introduction

You get called, offer your clammy hand, then lie and say, "It's great to be here." Nothing to it, you did it the last time you had a blind date. (Let's hope this goes a little better.)

Cliché time : you never get a second chance to make a first impression. Eye contact, a pleasant smile, and a firm handshake are paramount.

✣ Questions About You

The first part of the interview is all about "getting to know you." McKinsey calls it a PEI which stands for Personal Experience Interview. They will ask you to come up with several examples of times when you influenced or persuaded a group, about your relationship building style, and goals that you set for yourself and were successful in meeting. Interviewers will ask you several questions drawn from your resume (anything on your resume is fair game).

What they are looking for:

- a confident, comfortable demeanor and strong communication skills. (Are you a nervous wreck?)
- leadership ability and initiative. (Forget about the time you organized that keg party.)
- ability to be a team player. (Do you play well with others?)
- drive, aspirations, energy, morals, and ethics. (Do you have any?)

In this part of the interview you should be responding, not thinking. You're going to do enough thinking during the case questions to last you for a week. You need to research yourself beforehand. Look at the list of the most commonly asked questions in a consulting interview (*see sidebar*). You may not be asked any of these questions, but if you take the time to write out the answers, or better yet bullet point out the answers, you will be forced to think about things you haven't thought about in years (or ever). So dig into the old treasure chest and come up with memorable stories and accomplishments which substantiate the skills that will make you a strong candidate.

COMMONLY ASKED CONSULTING INTERVIEW QUESTIONS

If you take the time to answer these questions before the interview, you will be more articulate and focused when it comes time to perform.

- Tell me about yourself.
- What are you doing here?
- Why consulting?
- Why did you pick your school?
- What do you think consultants do?
- What do you know about this job and our firm?
- Why would you choose our firm over our competitors?
- How are your quantitative skills?
- What percentage is 7 of 63?
- Tell me of a time you showed leadership skills.
- Tell me of a time you were a team player.
- Give me an example of a time when you influence or persuaded a group.
- Tell me about a recent crisis you handled.
- Have you ever failed at anything?
- Tell me about a time that you took the initiative to start something.
- What type of work do you like to do best?
- With what other firms are you interviewing?
- Which other industries are you looking into?
- What accomplishments have given you the greatest satisfaction?
- What experiences/skills do you feel are particularly transferable to our organization?
- Why should I hire you?

Interviewers remember stories and accomplishments more than common answers ▶ ▶ ▶

You want to get labeled. If you tell the interviewer your captivating tale about windsurfing across the English Channel, then at the end of the day when the interviewer sees your name on her list she'll remember you as "the windsurfer." Everything you spoke about will come back to her. If she sees your name and thinks, "Which one was he?" your candidacy is over.

How Do I Answer? ▶ ▶ ▶

Three of the most problematic interview questions are :

- **Have you ever failed at anything?**
- **With what other firms are you interviewing?**
- **Within what other industries are you interviewing?**

How do you answer these truthfully?

Q : 1 **Have you ever failed at anything?**

Say yes! Everybody has failed at something. People fail all the time. That's how you learn.

• **Dos :** Do talk about a failure and what you learned from that failure. Better yet, talk about how you failed, what you learned from that mistake, then how you turned it into a success. A perfect example comes from Michael Jordan. He failed to make his high school basketball team his freshman year, persevered, and became a basketball legend. Have a story to tell; make it memorable.

* problem solving be-ed to can applied to all walks of life

A DOZEN REASONS TO ENTER CONSULTING

Just in case you're not sure, below are 13 (a baker's dozen) of the most popular reasons students go into consulting.

1. You'll work and learn from very intelligent and articulate people.
2. You'll develop a vast array of marketable skills in a prestigious environment.
3. The learning curve never ends.
4. You'll receive exposure to the corporate elite: the way they think, act, and analyze their problems.
5. You'll be exposed to many industries.
6. You'll work as part of a team.
7. You'll solve problems.
8. You'll make organizations more efficient.
9. You'll work on multiple projects.
10. You'll travel.
11. You'll improve your chances of being accepted into a top business school.
12. It will always look great on your resume.
13. The money's good.

• **Don'ts :** Don't talk about a personal failure. Stay away from anything that is going to make the interviewer feel uncomfortable (i.e., "I never got to straighten things out with my Dad before he passed away," or, "My girlfriend dumped me..."). Interviewers don't want to hear it. The other thing they don't want to hear is an academic failure. I can't tell you how many Harvard students have told me in mock interviews, "I took an upper-level science class, worked like a dog, but I failed." "What did you get in the class?" I'd ask. "B minus." That's not failing. If you really did fail a course, they would know about it and ask why it happened.

Q : 2 With what other firms are you interviewing?
It's okay to tell them that you're interviewing with other consulting firms. Competition's tough; you'd be foolish to put all your energy into just one firm. However, you must be able to tell them why they're your first choice and what makes them better in your mind than the other firms. Consulting firms are rated on a tier scale. There are first-tier firms and second- and third-tier firms. While who's in which tier is very subjective, don't be shy about mentioning interviews with other firms in either the same or higher tiers.

Q : 3 With what other industries are you interviewing?
Consulting goes hand in hand with two other industries. While interviewing for a consulting position, it's okay to mention that you are looking at investment banking and/or strategic planning. These positions look for the same qualities in a candidate and require similar job skills. In fact, McKinsey's and BCG's biggest competitor is Goldman Sachs–not one another.

+ Why Consulting?

You know the interviewer is going to ask you why you want to be a consultant. Now this is important–not only should your answer be immediate, but you must look the interviewer right in the eye. If you look away, it indicates that you are thinking about the question and that's enough to end the interview right then and there. You should have given this answer a great deal of thought long before you walked into the interview. While I don't want you to memorize your answer, I do want you to memorize bullet points. This makes your answer focused, linear, and an appropriate length. Avoid talking aimlessly. Having several good reasons why you want to be a consultant isn't enough. It's not always what you say, but how you say it. Your voice should carry sincerity and enthusiasm.

+ Possible Math Question

They may ask you about your quantitative skills. This could be followed by a small math question such as, "What's 100 divided by 7?" Or, "9 is what percentage of 72?" The questions aren't hard, but they might take you by surprise. It may be time to break out the flashcards.

*** Note :** *During the first part of the interview, you're being judged. The interviewer is asking herself whether or not she'd like to work and travel with you. Are you interesting? Engaging? Do you have a sense of humor and like to have fun? This is better known as the "airport test." The name comes from the question, "How would I feel if I were snowed in with this candidate for nine hours at the Buffalo Airport? Would we have a lot to talk about or would I have to pretend that I was in a coma so I wouldn't have to talk?"*

The interviewer is also measuring your maturity, poise, and communication skills, while thinking, "Would I feel comfortable bringing this candidate in front of a client?"

+ Case Questions

The second part of the interview is the case question(s). They carry a tremendous amount of weight. You can pass the airport test and be as poised and articulate as Cary Grant, but if you fumble the case, that's it. We'll cover the case questions in depth in Chapter Three.

+ Your Questions

The last part of the interview requires a good deal of research about both the industry and the company. In your research, you should be looking for answers to the pre-interview questions (*see sidebar*). Questions for which you can't locate answers become excellent questions to pose to your interviewer.

However, before you ask your first question, if there is anything critical that you didn't get a chance to bring up in the interview, now is the time. Simply state, "Before I ask my first question, I just want to make sure you understand...." Get it out before you leave the room. If you don't, you're going to kick yourself all the way home, and even worse, you'll never know if that statement could have turned the tide.

PRE-INTERVIEW QUESTIONS

1. What type of consulting does the firm do?
2. What industries does the firm specialize in?
3. How big is the firm?
   - How many domestic and international offices does the firm have?
   - How many professionals are in the firm?
4. What kinds of training programs does the firm offer?
5. What type of work does an entry-level consultant do?
6. How much client contact does an entry-level consultant have the first year?
7. Does the firm have a mentor program?
8. How often do first-years sleep in their own beds? What's their travel schedule like?
9. How many hours make-up a typical workday?
10. How is a case team picked?
11. How often do you get reviewed?
12. How many consultants does the firm expect to hire this year?
13. How does that compare to last year?
14. Where do the consultants go when they leave the firm?
15. Is it possible to transfer to other offices, even international offices?

The best ways to collect these answers are to ▸▸▸

- ☐ **Attend career fairs and speak to the firm representatives :** Pull out your list of questions and ask three or four. Make sure that you try to turn this meeting into a conversation. At the end, thank the reps for their time, ask them for their business cards, and inquire whether it would be all right if you called or emailed them with further questions. At this point, no one is going to judge you on your level of company knowledge. They are there to provide information and to hype the firm.

- ☐ **Scour the company's web site :** This will let you know how the firm sees itself and the image that it's trying to project.

- ☐ **Talk to alumni and graduate school students who used to work for the companies that you're interviewing with :** Often career services offices will be able to match you up with alumni who are working in a specific industry. Interviewing past employees can be very enlightening. They will tell you more about their old firm in a half an hour than you'll learn by spending two hours on the Internet. Plus they'll tell you things that you'll never find on the Internet. They can be completely objective; they don't have to try to sell the firm.

- ☐ **Attend company information meetings :** Get your name and face in front of firm representatives, so that they can associate your face with your resume. While these people don't have the power to hire you, they do have the power to get you on the interview list. Top-tier firms often get 400 resumes for 100 first-round interview slots. Ensure that interview slot by networking and schmoozing with firm representatives every chance you get. One of the best kept secrets of company presentations is to go early. If a company presentation is scheduled to start at 6 pm show up at 5:45. Most students won't arrive until 6 or a little after, but the firm's representatives show up at around 5:30 to make sure that the room is set up correctly and the cheese table is laid out nicely. If you show up early, not only will it impress the consultants, but it will allow you to get at least five minutes of quality face time with one of them. They are more likely to remember you if you talk for five minutes in the beginning of the night than if you hang around until the end hoping for 45 seconds of their time. They are also more likely to have their business card with them. Remember to ask for their business card and send a follow-up email.

- ☐ **Search *The Wall Street Journal* or Lexis-Nexis for articles on the firm :** This allows you to be current on any firm's news.

Have your list of questions with any specific facts or figures you've dug up written out when you walk into the interview. It shows that you have done your homework and have given this interview a great deal of thought. Besides, if you freeze up, it's all right there in front of you.

✢ The Grand Finale : Why Should I Hire You?

This is your opportunity to shine and market yourself. But before you launch into a laundry list of skills and attributes, you may want to simply state that they should hire you because you want to be a consultant. Then reiterate all the reasons why that you brought up earlier when they asked you, "Why consulting?"

Consulting firms look for "low-risk" hires. You're a low-risk hire if you've worked in consulting, liked it, and want to return, or if you've done your homework. Consulting firms' biggest fear is that they will spend a lot of time and money hiring and training you, only to have you bail out after six months because consulting isn't what you expected it to be.

If they aren't convinced that this is what you want to do, then it doesn't matter how talented you are. It's not worth it for them to extend you an offer. Think of it this way: How would you feel if someone accepted your dinner invitation because their first choice fell through? If your heart's not in it, they don't want you.

Students who receive job offers in consulting do so for four reasons ▶ ▶ ▶

1. They are able to convince the interviewer that they are committed to consulting and know what they're getting into (e.g., type of work, lifestyle, travel).
2. They can demonstrate success-oriented behavior.
3. They exhibit good analytical skills when answering case questions. (That's where we come in.)
4. They are able to articulate their thoughts, create a positive presence, and defend themselves without being defensive.

Now that you understand the structure of the interview for the first round, the subsequent rounds are not all that different. The second round is often held at a nearby hotel and usually consists of two interviews, both 45 minutes in length, each with a heavy focus on case questions. The third round is typically held in the firm's offices where there are five interviews, 45 to 60 minutes each, again with a heavy emphasis on case questions.

One last note on preparation : Be familiar with business terms and trends. No firm is going to judge you on your business acumen, but if you can't define profit and loss, revenues, fixed and variable costs, or cost-benefit analysis, then start reading. (Please refer to the Consulting Buzzwords section.) You should also read *The Wall Street Journal* every day to keep abreast of national and world news. In other words, climb out of that academic shell and join the rest of the world. Your familiarity with business terms and trends will make it easier for you to communicate with the interviewer and demonstrate your interest in business and consulting.

And now, at last, it's time for...

WHAT FIRMS LOOK FOR

Consultants spend a great deal of their time on the road at the client's site. They work in small teams and are sometimes put in charge of groups of the clients' employees. Often, consultants work under great pressure in turbulent environments while dealing with seemingly unmanageable problems. It takes a certain type of personality to remain cool under pressure, to influence the client without being condescending, and to be both articulate and analytical at the same time.

As we said earlier, the business of consulting is really the renting of brains, packaged and delivered with an engaging and confident personality. So as you work through the case, the interviewer is asking herself, Is the candidate:

- relaxed, confident, and mature?
- a good listener?
- engaging and enthusiastic?
- exhibiting strong social and presentation skills?
- asking insightful and probing questions?
- able to determine what's truly relevant?
- organizing the information effectively and developing a logical framework for analysis?
- stating assumptions clearly?
- comfortable discussing the multifunctional aspects of the case?
- trying to quantify his response at every opportunity?
- displaying both business sense & common sense?
- thinking creatively?

A case question is a fun, intriguing, and active interviewing tool used to evaluate the multi-dimensional aspects of a candidate.

+ Purpose of the Case Question

Interviewers don't ask case questions to embarrass and humiliate you. They don't ask case questions to see you sweat and squirm (although some might consider it a side perk). They do ask case questions...

- to test your analytical ability
- to test your ability to think logically and organize your answer
- to observe your thought process
- to test your tolerance for ambiguity and data overload
- to assess your poise, self-confidence, and communication skills under pressure
- to discover your personality
- to see if you're genuinely intrigued by problem solving
- to determine if consulting is a good "fit" for you

+ Case Preparation

Case questions can be made simple through preparation and practice. I never like to equate an interview with a test. But they do have in common the fact that the more you prepare, the better you'll do. Maybe you've experienced the feeling of being so prepared for an exam that you can't wait for the professor to hand it out so you can rip right through it. Case questions are the same way. Firms look to see if you have that "rip right through it" look in your eyes. It's called confidence.

Before we look at some cases, it is best to understand the Commandments. Follow these rules and your case interviewing life will become much easier.

✛ The Case Commandments

[1. Listen to the Question]

Listening is the most important skill a consultant has. The case isn't about you or the consultant; it's about the client. What are they really asking for? Pay particular attention to the last sentence–one word can change the entire case.

[2. Take Notes]

Taking notes during the case interview allows you to check back with the facts of the case. As someone once said, "The weakest ink is stronger than the best memory." If you blank out, all the information is right in front of you.

[3. Summarize the Question]

After you are given the question, take a moment to summarize the highlights (out loud):

- it shows the interviewer that you listened
- it allows you to hear the information a second time
- it keeps you from answering the wrong question
- it fills that otherwise awkward pause when you're trying to think of something intelligent to say

[4. Verify the Objective(s)]

Professional consultants always ask their clients to verify their objective(s). Even if the objective seems obvious, there could be an additional, underlying objective. When the objective seems apparent, phrase the question differently: "One objective is to increase sales. Are there any other objectives I should know about?"

[5. Ask Clarifying Questions]

You ask questions for three main reasons:

- to get additional information that will help you identify and label the question
- to demonstrate to the interviewer that you are not shy about asking probing questions under difficult circumstances (something you'll be doing on a regular basis as a consultant)
- to turn the question into a conversation. Nothing turns off an interviewer quicker than a five-minute monologue

In the beginning of the case you have more latitude in your questioning. You should ask basic questions about the company, the industry, the competition, external market factors, and the product. The further you get into the case, the more your questions should switch from open-ended questions to closed-ended questions. You start to get into trouble when you ask broad, sweeping questions that are hard for the interviewer to answer. These kinds of questions give the impression that you're trying to get the interviewer to answer the case for you.

[6. Organize Your Answer]

Identify and label your case, then lay out your structure. This is the hardest part of a case–and the most crucial. It drives your case and is often the major reason behind whether you get called back. We will spend more time on this in Chapter Four.

[7. Hold that Thought for "One Alligator"]

The interviewer wants you to think out loud, but think before you speak. If you make a statement that is way off-base in an interview, the recruiter will wonder if he can trust you in front of a client.

[8. Manage Your Time]

Your answer should be as linear as possible. Don't get bogged down in the details. Answer from a macro-level and move the answer forward. It's easy to lose your way by going off on a tangent. Stay focused on what the original question asked.

[9. By the Numbers]

If possible, try to work numbers into the problem. Demonstrate that you think quantitatively and that you are comfortable with numbers.

[10. Be Coachable]

Listen to the interviewer's feedback. Is she trying to guide you back on track? Pay attention to her body language. Are you boring her? Is she about to nod off? Is she enthralled?

Being coachable also means asking for help when you need it. If you run into a wall, lose your train of thought, or are just in over your head, ask for help. There is no shame in asking for help–it's a sign of maturity. Look at it from the interviewer's point of view. If you were working on an actual project and got stuck, she would much rather have you ask for help than waste time spinning your wheels.

[11. Be Creative and Brainstorm]

Some of the best experiences you'll have as a consultant will be brainstorming over Chinese food at 10 o'clock at night. *Brainstorming without commitment*, as consultants call it, allows you to toss out uninhibited suggestions without being married to them. It gives you the opportunity to review all the options and eliminate the inappropriate ones. Consulting firms like liberal arts candidates with intellectual curiosity who can "think outside the box" and offer up a new and interesting perspective.

[12. Exude Enthusiasm and a Positive Attitude]

Earlier we spoke about a "ripping right through it" attitude. It's not enough to do well on the case, you have to thrive on the challenge of the case. Recruiters want people who are excited by problem solving and can carry that enthusiasm throughout the entire interview.

[13. Bring Closure and Summarize]

If you have done all of the above and you've made it through the analysis, the final action is to create a sense of closure by summarizing the case. Review your findings, restate your suggestions, and make a recommendation. You don't need to sum up the whole answer; pick two or three key points and touch on those. Students are often afraid to make a recommendation, thinking that their analysis was faulty so therefore their answers will be wrong. There are no wrong answers. Just make sure your answer makes good business sense and common sense.

+ Types of Case Questions

Case questions generally fall into one of three major categories: brainteasers, back-of-the-envelope questions, which are often called market-sizing questions, and business case questions. It's quite common to find a market-sizing question enclosed within a larger business case question. Whether fun or frustrating, all case questions are valuable learning experiences.

Brainteasers

Brainteasers are scarce these days, but they still pop up in the occasional first-round interview, so it's important to be aware of them. Brainteasers are basically the same riddles and conundrums that we've all been struggling to solve since fourth grade. Some brainteasers have a definite answer; others are more flexible in their solutions. Interviewers are looking to see not only if you can come up with a good answer, but also whether you can handle the pressure. Do you get frustrated, stressed, and upset? The key is to keep your cool and try to break the problem down logically. Just give it your best shot, and don't be afraid to laugh at your mistakes or be a bit self-deprecating. It makes you human and more fun to be with.

Below is an example of a brainteaser with a definite answer, and one with a more flexible solution.

The Bags of Gold

Q : 1 ***There are three bags of gold. One of the bags contains fake gold. All the bags and all the coins look exactly alike. There is the same number of coins in each bag. The real gold coins weigh one ounce each, the fake coins weigh 1.1 oz apiece. You have a penny scale and one penny, which means you can weigh something just once. (You load the scale, put the penny in, and the scale spits out a piece of paper with the weight.) How can you tell which bag has the fake gold?***

A : 1 *You take one coin from the first bag of gold, two coins from the second bag, and three coins from the third bag. Place them all on the scale. If the coins weigh 6.1 oz, then you know that the first bag held the fake gold. If they weighed 6.2 oz, then it was the second bag. If the coins weighed 6.3 oz, then the third bag held the gold.*

Virgin Atlantic

Q : 2 ***You are driving down the road in a mini-van. In the back of the van are six 8-year-olds who you are bringing back from soccer practice. None of the children are yours. You drive by a Virgin Atlantic billboard featuring Austin Powers with the caption, "There's only one Virgin on this billboard, baby." One of the children asks, "What's a virgin?" What do you tell her?***

A : 2 *Obviously, there is no right answer. People have come up with anything from grades of olive oil to airplane logos to "Ask your mother." Again, the key is to prove that you can remain poised. As a father, I can tell you what I'd say: "Who wants ice cream?!"*

There are numerous puzzle and brainteaser books to be found in your local bookstore. If you are worried about these types of questions, you may want to pick up one of these books.

Back-of-the-Envelope

Back-of-the-envelope questions or market-sizing questions surface all the time and can be found during any round of interviews and within many larger business case questions. The back-of-the-envelope question received its name because the questions used to start with, "You're on an airplane, with no books, phone, or any other resources. On the back of an envelope figure...." You'll find some of these questions intriguing; some will be fun; others preposterous. However, it's important to have the "rip right through it" look in your eyes; at least pretend that you're having fun.

Oftentimes during market-sizing questions all you have to work with are assumptions. There are going to be instances when your assumptions are wrong. Sometimes the interviewer will correct you, other times he will let it go. The interviewer is more interested in your logic and thought process than whether your answer is correct. If you are still concerned you can always say, "I'm not that familiar with this market, so if my assumptions are off, please correct me." Ninety percent of the time the interviewer will tell you not to worry about it. Everything you say has the potential to be questioned – be ready to stand behind your assumptions. Your assumptions should be based in some sort of logic. If you just pull them out of the air you're risking the interviewer aggressively challenging your assumptions and your credibility.Examples are:

- **How many gas stations are there in the U.S.?**
- **How many garden hoses were sold in the U.S. last year?**
- **How many pairs of boxers are sold in the U.S. each year?**
- **How much does a 747 weigh?**

Although they seem similar, these are four very different questions. Here are some hints.

- First of all, there are no right answers. Even if you had just read a Forbes article on the number of gas stations and could recite the exact total, the consultants wouldn't care. They want to see how logically you answer the question.
- All you really have to work with are assumptions. If your assumptions are too far off then the interviewer will tell you; otherwise, guesstimate.

- Use easy numbers–round up or down.
- Write the numbers down. Half of your brain is trying to figure out how best to answer this question and the other half is trying to remember the sum you just figured. Write the numbers down so you can focus on the process, not the numbers.
- Determine if this is a population-based question, a household question, an individual question, or a "Who thinks this stuff up?" question. To determine whether it's a population, household, or individual question, ask yourself if the item is used by a population, a household, or an individual.

BACK-OF-THE-ENVELOPE AND MARKET-SIZING ASSUMPTIONS

Oftentimes with back-of-the-envelope questions all you really have to work with are assumptions. Below are common assumptions.

- The population of the United States is 280 million, although this number can fluctuate from 250 million to 300 million to make your calculations easier.
- Men and women each represent 50% of the U.S. population.
- The average life expectancy of an American is around 75 years.
- Americans per household is 2.8.
- Number of U.S. households is 100 million.
- Percentage of households that own a VCR is 90 percent.
- Percentage of households that have cable TV is 90 percent.
- Percentage of households that have a PC is 60 percent.
- Percentage of households that are connected to the Internet is 76 percent.

❑ **How many gas stations are there in the U.S.? (Population question)**

I live in a town with a population of 30,000. There are six gas stations serving our town. Therefore, I'll assume that each gas station serves about 5,000 customers. If the population of the U.S. is 280 million, I'll just divide 280 million by 5,000 and get 56,000 gas stations in the U.S.

If you tried to answer this question based on households or individuals you would quickly find yourself mired in numerous and unnecessary calculations.

❑ **How many garden hoses were sold in the U.S. last year? (Household question)**

The population of the U.S. is 280 million people. The average U.S. household is made up of 2.8 people so we are talking about 100 million households.

I'm going to estimate that 50 percent of the households are either suburban or rural. That makes 50 million households. I'll also assume that 20 percent of those homes are apartments or condos. That narrows us down to 40 million houses which most likely use a garden hose. Garden hoses are relatively inexpensive so people are likely to have a hose in the front and a hose in the back yard. That makes 80 million hoses. I want to add in another 10 million hoses which can be found in nurseries, zoos, and other outdoor facilities like Fenway Park. Most of those businesses have at least two hoses.

We are now up to 90 million garden hoses. Hoses aren't replaced every year. I'd say that they are replaced every 3 years unless they are run over by a lawn mower or run into the business end of a dog's tooth. So we take 90 million hoses divide it by 3 and come up with 30 million garden hoses sold each year.

❑ **How many pairs of boxers are sold in the U.S. each year? (Individual question)**

I'm going to start by stating some assumptions. I'm going to assume that the population of the U.S. is 250 million, that the life expectancy is 80 years, and that there are the same number of people in each age group (i.e., there is the exact same number of 3-year-olds as 73-year-olds). So if you divide 250 million by 80, you get a little over 3 million people per age group. We'll round it off to 3 million people. I will also assume a 50/50 split between men and women.

Children ages zero–three mostly wear diapers, and kids ages four–nine mainly wear jockey-style. So we'll focus on the ages between 10 and 80. That's 70 years to cover. I'm going to go out on a limb here and say that only 10% of females ages 10 to 30 own a pair of boxers and, of that group, each might buy one pair a year.

So :
(1.5 million females x 20 years) x 10% = **3 million boxers.**

Males between the ages of 10 and 20 wear them as a fashion statement, so I'll assume that 75% wear boxers and that they buy 3 pairs a year (the economical 3-pack).

So :
(1.5 million males x 10 years) x 75% = 11,250,000 million boxers
11 million boxers x 3 pairs = **33 million boxers.**

Of males between the ages of 21 and 80 (round off to 60 years), 50% wear boxers and buy or receive as birthday or holiday gifts 6 pairs (2 sets of 3-packs) a year.

So :
(1.5 males x 60 years) x 50% = 15 million males wearing boxers.
15 million x 6 pairs of boxers = **90 million pairs of boxers.**

Add them all together :
3 million + 33 million + 90 million = 126 million pairs of boxer shorts were sold in the U.S. last year.

❑ **How much does a 747 weigh? ("Who thinks this stuff up?" question.)**

Your guess is as good as mine. Ask questions, then break down the elements, and make assumptions. Are there passengers on board? No. Any baggage? No. Are the fuel tanks full or empty? Full. Any food or beverages on board? No.

Now you just go ahead and calculate the weight of each part of the plane.

- **8 full fuel tanks :** I'll assume the plane can fly 6,000 miles and uses 10 gallons to the mile. So that's 60,000 gallons at 2 pounds a gallon equals 120,000 pounds.
- **18 tires :** I'll assume that the tires weigh 200 pounds each–that's 3,600 pounds.
- **4 engines :** I'll assume 2,500 pounds each adds another 10,000 pounds.
- **2 wings :** 200 feet long by 30 feet wide is 6,000 square feet, times a square foot weight of 5 pounds times 2 wings equals 60,000 pounds.
- **Interior :** 75 rows of seats times 4 feet per row equals 300 feet. Add on the cockpit, bathrooms, etc., so let's say around 400 feet long. I assume that the average weight per foot is 10 pounds, which equals 4,000 pounds.

• **The seats :** They number, say 500, and weigh 10 pounds each, so that's 5,000 pounds.

• And because the **air in the cabin** doesn't flow through, it's captured air so we need to add one ton for the air in the cabin–2,000 pounds.

• The **aluminum exterior** is pretty thin and lightweight. If the plane is 400 feet long by 25 feet high, then about 10,000 exterior square feet at 1 pound per foot equals 10,000 pounds.

• **Miscellaneous materials** including the tail, overhead bins, carpet, stairs and bathroom fixtures add on, say, another 2,000 pounds.

Then you add up the pieces.
120,000 + 3,600 + 10,000 + 60,000 + 4,000 + 5,000 + 2,000 + 2,000 + 10,000 = 216,000, or round up to 220,000 pounds, or **110 tons**.

❑ **Estimate the 2004 dollar amount of the on-line grocery market in the U.S.? (Household problem)**

• There are 280 million Americans and the average household is 2.8 people, equaling 100 million households. In order to use this service one needs access to a computer and the Internet.

• Sixty percent of all households have a computer and 50 percent are connected to the Internet. So that means 50 million households have Internet access. There is a minimum order size of $100 in order to get free delivery.

• Therefore, I'll assume that 5 percent of the households use it. That equals 2.5 million homes. In our family we spend $150 dollars a week. There are four of us, including two small children, so I'll estimate the average grocery bill to be around the minimum at $100 a week or $400 a month.

• So we have 2.5 million homes ordering $400 of groceries a month or $4,800 a year. I'll round up to $5,000 a year. However, they probably only order half their groceries on-line. So you have 2.5 million homes ordering $2,500 of groceries. That equals $6.25 billion a year.

❑ **How much chocolate did America eat in 2004? (Individual problem)**

First, I'm going to determine what percentage of the population loves chocolate; what percentage likes chocolate; and what percentage doesn't care for it, is allergic to it or is too young to eat it. Then I'm going to look at how they eat it.

• I'll assume that there are 250 million Americans.[1]

30% love chocolate – 75 million
50% like chocolate – 125 million
20% don't care for it – 50 million

• People consume chocolate in the following ways, via candy, junk food, commercial baking, coffees, chocolate milk and adult drinks (i.e., B52s). Taking into account four crucial holidays, Valentine's Day, Easter, Halloween, and Christmas I'm going to estimate the number of pounds of chocolate each person within those categories eats a year.

• I'll assume that the average candy bar weighs 1.5 ounces. Someone who loves chocolate probably eats 2 candy bars a week (3 oz. times 52 weeks) equals 156 oz. or round it off to 160 oz. or 10 pounds. The person who likes chocolate probably eats two candy bars a month (3 oz. times 12 months) equals 24 oz. Or 1.5 pounds. We'll round it off to 2 pounds.

The person who doesn't care for probably won't eat any candy bars.

• Next let's look at commercial baking. It's hard to get away from chocolate, it seems to turn up everywhere. This area includes desserts at restaurants, special coffee drinks, hot chocolate and junk food. Someone who loves chocolate probably consumes another 5 pounds while someone who likes it might eat another pound. I'm also going to add one pound for those who don't care for it. They might consume it in ways that they don't know about or eat a piece of birthday cake, that sort of thing.

• Finally, ice cream and homemade items like cookies and cakes. While these items aren't solid chocolate people probably consume more goodies containing less pure chocolate.

• People who love chocolate eat 25 pounds times 75 million equals 1.875 billion pounds. People who like chocolate consume 8 pounds times 125 million equals 1 billion pounds. And people who don't care for chocolate eat 1 pound times 50 million equals 50 million pounds. This all adds up to 2.9 or around 3 billion pounds of chocolate.

	Loves	Likes	Doesn't care
Candy	10 lbs.	2 lb.	0
Commercial baking / coffees / drinks	5 lbs.	1 lb.	1 lb.
Ice cream / homemade cookies	10 lbs.	5 lbs.	0

NB. (Americans consumed approximately 3.5 billion pounds of chocolate in 2000.).

❑ **Estimate the size of the bubble gum market in the U.S.**
(General population question.)

I'm going to make a few assumptions first. I'll assume that there are 280 million Americans and that the average life expectancy of an American is 80 years. I'm also going to assume that there is an even number of people in each age category. So I divide 280 million by 80 and get 3.5 million people in each age group. To make things easier, I'm going to calculate assuming 50 weeks in a year.

I'd also like to think about where bubble gum is sold. As I remember, bubble gum is sold in packs of 10 pieces in convenience stores, grocery stores, newsstands, etc. You can also find bubble gum inside baseball trading cards, and gumball machines.

I'm going to break the population down into different age categories. Estimate the number of people that chew bubble gum in each age group, the number of pieces they chew each week and convert that into an annual number. Let's make a chart.

So I'm going to say that 20 billion pieces of bubble gum are sold each year. Ten pieces per pack equals 2 billion packs at 50 cents a pack equals $1 billion.

Ages	No. People	# that Chew	pieces / per week	pieces / year
0–5	17.5	1m	2	100m
6–10	17.5	12m	10	6b
11–15	17.5	12m	20	12b
16–20	17.5	10m	5	2.5b
21_40	70	4m	1	200m
40–80	140	1m	1	50m
Totals	280 m	40m		20.85b

❑ **How many ATM's are there in the country? (Population problem)**

I live in Needham, Massachusetts. The population of my town is approximately 30,000. There are fifteen ATMs in town. So I'll assume that each ATM services 2,000 people. I'm going to assume that the population of the U.S. is around 280 million people. Next I'll divide 2,000 into 280 million and come up with 140,000 ATMs.

▶ Business Case Questions

Business case questions come in all shapes and sizes, but they usually fall into two categories : numbers cases, and business strategy and operations cases.

❑ **Numbers Cases** : There are pure number cases that are really just math problems that you are expected to do in your head. There are also "case-like" numbers cases, which seem like strategy cases, but are not. Case-like number cases are about numbers–sounds simple, but most people get them wrong because they don't listen to the question and try to turn it into a strategy case.

- **Pure number cases to do in your head :**

A) The total widget market is $170 million, and our sales are $30 million. What percentage of the market share do we hold?

B) Our total manufacturing costs are $20 million. With that we can make 39,379 units. What is our approximate cost per unit?

C) Our total costs are $75,000. Labor costs make up 25% of the total costs. How much are our labor costs?

D) You bought a stock for $36 a share. Today it jumped 6%. How much is your stock worth?

E) You raised $3.5 million for a start-up. Your commission is 2.5%. What's your commission in dollars?

F) What's 7 times 45?

G) In 1999, the number of current outstanding shares for Macromedia Inc. was 41,084,000. Institutional investors hold 25,171,000. Approximately, what is the percentage of shares held by institutions?

Answers : A) about 18% B) about $500 C) $18,750 D) $38.16 E) $87,500 F) 315 G) 60%

• **Case-like number cases :**

American Express is facing stiff competition from a host of new credit cards that have no annual fee and low interest rates. In response, American Express is considering dropping its $50 annual fee. What are the economics of dropping the $50 fee? (This is a popular case and one that has repeatedly turned up in interviews.)

Nine out of 10 students think this case is about competition. They focus their answer on strategy and alternatives to dropping the fee. The first part of this question is not relevant. The real question is **"What are the economics of dropping the $50 fee?"**

In order to answer this question you need to ask three questions:

- How many card members does Amex have?
- What is the average amount that each card member spends annually?
- What are Amex's revenue streams?

Amex has 10 million card members. Amex card members average $2,000 a year in purchases. Amex makes 2% from each purchase.

Amex Revenues :

10 million customers paying a $50 annual fee equals $500 million. Each member spends $2,000 x 2% = $40 a year x 10 million customers = $400 million. Total revenues then = $900 million, with 55% of that figure coming from fees.

Would card members spend more money if they didn't have to pay the annual fee? Amex card members would have to more than double their purchases to make up for the loss in fee revenues. It seems unlikely that they would go from spending $2,000 a year to spending $5,000 a year because of a dropped $50 fee.

Even a modest bump in new members couldn't make up the difference.

How many new customers would Amex have to secure in order to make up the $500 million dollar difference? Amex would have to more than double its card members from 10 million to about 25 million in a short period, say two years. Is that feasible? It took Amex 25 years to reach the 10 million customer base. So doubling it in two years seems unrealistic.

My advice to Amex is to keep its fee in place.

That's it. That's the answer. The interviewer doesn't want to hear about reducing the fee to $25 or turning Amex into a credit card. This is a straightforward question. Listen to the question.

❑ **Business Strategy and Operations Cases :** Some business strategy and operations cases should be answered in less than 15 minutes. These are referred to as mini-cases. An example:

> • *GE has invented a new light bulb that never burns out. It could burn for more than 500 years and it would never blink. The director of marketing calls you into her office and asks, "How would you price this?" What do you tell her?* *(See answer on pg 103.)*

A regular case question, like the DuPont case below, could take anywhere from 30 to 45 minutes to answer. It could combine a market-sizing question with a strategy question all rolled into one, such as:

- *DuPont has just invented a lightweight, super-absorbent, biodegradable material that would be perfect for disposable diapers. What do they do with it? (See answer on pg 123.)*

Written Case Questions and Tests

Over the last couple of years we have seen more and more firms turn to written cases, particularly in the second and third rounds. Monitor Group was the first to pioneer the written case. Since then they have added a few new twists to the process. The interview can go something like this:

You arrive for the interview and are handed a written case (usually about 5 pages; three pages of text and two pages of charts and graphs). You are given twenty to thirty minutes to read and take notes. When the time is up, a consultant comes in and you are expected to "present" the case, much like in a Harvard Business School class. More often than not it turns into a discussion. Chances are you will be touching on all the same points as you would if given a verbal case.

Here's where it gets really interesting. Sometimes when you have finished reading the case you are taken into a room where you'll meet two to three other candidates (you all have read the same case and are applying for the same position). Again, you are expected to "present" the case. The consultants watch closely to see how you interact with the other candidates. Are you dominating the discussion? Are you sitting back and being dominated by others? Or are you building on what the other candidates say in a positive and civil manner. The Monitor consultants look to see how you interact with your peers. Are you a team player? Do you play well with others? Can you hold your own? It all boils down to fit, communication skills, respect for others, empathy and teamwork.

This is taking the brilliance of case questions as an interviewing tool one step further.

There could be one last twist. Sometimes when you arrive you are joined by two or three other candidates in a small conference room. You are all given the same case and asked to present it in twenty minutes. A Monitor consultant stays in the conference room with you to monitor the group's interaction and dynamics while accessing the leadership skills of all the candidates. When your team is ready to present, two other consultants join in and your "team" presents the case.

Now one, two or all three of the candidates might be called back for the next round. While you act as part of a team during presentation of the case, you are all judged individually.

McKinsey & Company now requires that some candidates take a written test. "The test is testing problem solving in a written format; folks will be surprised that the straight 'quant' questions are the minority. It's not like a GRE quant test," explains a senior McKinsey recruiter.

"The bulk of it involves making judgment calls/recommendations based on information available to you at that point," the recruiter explains. "The exercise is supposed to feel like a case interview, but with multiple choice responses."

There are three cases based on McKinsey engagements - 35 questions total, about 12 per case. Candidates receive a bit more information about the business, the environment and the problem with each question.

Students get 70 minutes and can't bring in calculators or scratch paper. The test was designed by ETS (the SAT and GMAT folks). "It was fun, now that it's over," recants a non-MBA Harvard graduate student. "There are some ratios and percentages, a couple formulas, but nothing too overwhelming. Also a few charts are used to present some of the information, but again fairly basic, in my opinion."

A McKinsey recruiter states "You need to be comfortable with calculating some percentages, basic equations, understanding relationships among data, but nothing terribly advanced."

Some international offices have a math section that one student says is more like the GMAT than the GRE. You have 18 questions and get 30 minutes to complete it. "You start with probability and it gets harder from there," recounts a Harvard graduate student.

The McKinsey recruiter explains, "The resulting score is used as one more 'data point' on problem solving for the interviewers to refer to if they have concerns or opposing reads. There is no magic or required score, and performance in face-to-face interviews are of greater importance to us."

Reading Charts and Graphs. One of the best ways to shake the dust off your chart and graph reading is to look at the charts and graphs printed in *The Wall Street Journal* and *The Economist* and draw some conclusions. Then read the article and compare your thoughts to the main points of the article.

Making Slides. There is another new twist this year, making slides. The recruiter hands you a few pages of data and asks that you create (on paper) three or four PowerPoint® slides. You are then expected to present them during the case as you would during a presentation to a client.

+ Irking the Interviewer

Interviewers get easily bored and irked. Let's face it, these guys and gals spend most of their days telling the CEOs of Fortune 1,000,000 companies what to do. Now, they've been yanked out of a really important assignment to interview you and a dozen of your closest friends. Yawn... "I postponed my meeting with Bill Gates for this? Dazzle me!"

The first step toward CID (Case Interview Dazzlement) is to avoid costly and obvious mistakes. Listed below are the most common mistakes that past interviewees (some still unemployed) made.

❑ **The Leno / Letterman syndrome**
A five-minute monologue will do more to hurt your career than any of the other mistakes. Remember, you ask questions not only to get additional information, but to draw the interviewer into the case with you. Make the interviewer feel that he is a stakeholder in your candidacy. Turn the question into a conversation.

❑ **What was the question again?**
Listen to the question; write it down; then repeat it to the interviewer. Candidates are always answering the wrong question because they don't take the time to identify what the interviewer is really asking. Listen to the question!

❑ **Explosion of the mouth**
I see it all the time, people can't give me the answer fast enough. Slow down. Don't jump off the mark and give the first answer that pops into your head. Take your time and analyze the information. The interviewer is there to observe the logic and thought process behind your answer.

❑ **Digression city**
You go off on a tangent because it's easy, you're on a roll, and it provides you with a false sense of security. You think it hides the fact that you can't move forward in your answer, but it doesn't. Tangents take you off the path and it becomes extremely difficult to get back on the straight and narrow.

A case question is like a long corridor with numerous side doors. Suppose the question was, "How do we increase sales for the local 7-Eleven convenience store?" You start walking down the corridor and you open the first door on the right and yell, "We can raise our prices." Close the door and move on to the next door. Open that door and yell, "We need to get more people in the store." Close the door and move on.

The problem arises when you open the door and yell, "We need to get more people in the store." Then you start walking down the side hall trying to come up with creative ways to get more people in the door. You come up with all sorts of promotions involving your favorite late-night snack food. Hey, this is easy! But that's NOT the question.

❑ **Trying to bull your way through a consulting china cabinet**
Don't use terms that you don't understand fully. Throwing out a buzzword or business term in the wrong context highlights the fact that you have a nasty habit of discussing things about which you know little. If you do that in an interview, what will you do in front of a client?

❑ **Asking open-ended questions**
Open-ended questions that try to get the interviewer to answer the case for you will irk the interviewer, big time. It is far better to make assumptions than to ask the interviewer for the answer. An example would be if you were reviewing labor costs.

Right : Because the economy is strong and there are plenty of jobs, I'll assume that our labor costs have gone up.

Wrong : What has been going on with our labor costs?

+ The Trouble with Math

Do you have trouble doing math in your head? Are you often off by zeros? When I do case interviews with students, the most common problem is basic math. It's the zeros that students have trouble with. From Ph.D.s to undergraduates, it's the zeros.

Number Table[1]

	10	100	1,000	10,000	100,000
10	100	1,000	10,000	100,000	1,000,000
100	1,000	10,000	100,000	1,000,000	10,000,000
1,000	10,000	100,000	1,000,000	10,000,000	100,000,000
10,000	100,000	1,000,000	10,000,000	100,000,000	1,000,000,000
100,000	1,000,000	10,000,000	100,000,000	1,000,000,000	
	1,000,000	10,000,000	100,000,000	1,000,000,000	

1 Number Table produced and designed by Maria Teresa Petersen Harvard MPP '01.

+ Best Case Thinking

In my years of training Harvard students to answer case questions, I've realized that the major problem many of my students have is simply getting started. Sometimes they're overwhelmed, sometimes they're nervous, and sometimes they just don't have a clue. So in 1996, with the help of a student, I developed the Tomensen/Cosentino Case Framework. Over the years it has been successfully tested in thousands of case interviews. After hundreds of debriefings, I have refined it, simplified it, and renamed it. But the biggest change is that I turned it from a framework into a system, The Ivy Case System.

A framework is a structure that helps you organize your thoughts and analyze the case in a logical manner. Often, however, you have to cut and paste from a number of frameworks in order to answer any single case question. As I've mentioned, the difference between a framework and a system is that a framework is really a tool, while a system is a process. Instead of memorizing seven individual frameworks and then trying to decide which one(s) to apply, you learn the system, which already has the tools built in.

The Ivy Case System is a two-part system made up of four easy steps to get you going and 11 popular case scenarios (*see sidebar*), each equipped with a collection of ideas and questions that will help you structure the remainder of your response. If you follow through the outline I've given for each scenario, you can be confident that your response will be logical and cohesive.

These first four steps will provide you with a quick start (no long, awkward pause between question and answer). They'll get you five minutes into the question, give you momentum, and provide you with enough information to decide which of the 11 case scenarios (or whatever combination thereof) is most appropriate to the case question at hand. You will recognize the four steps from the "Key Guidelines" section.

You may want to read through the following explanation of the Ivy Case System and then check out a practice case or two to see how the system can be applied. Then it will be time to revisit the system and learn it.

The interviewer has just finished giving you the case. Here's what you do!

THE ELEVEN CASE SCENARIOS

Business cases traditionally have focused on either business strategy or business operations. However, with today's more complex cases, candidates are getting case questions that cover both categories and multiple scenarios.

Strategy Scenarios :

1. Entering a new market
2. Mergers and Acquisitions
3. Developing a new product
4. Pricing strategies
5. Growth strategies
6. Starting a new business
7. Competitive response

Operations Scenarios :

8. Increasing sales
9. Reducing costs
10. Improving the bottom line
11. Turnarounds

When operations cases are really about strategy (e.g., Strategy : Should we proceed with a turnaround? vs. Operations : How do we proceed with a turnaround?) then think about using cost-benefit analysis (in which you analyze the pros and cons of each possibility).

✢ The First Four Steps

[1. Summarize the Question]

It shows the interviewer that you listened. It allows you to hear the information again, and it keeps you from answering the wrong question. When listening to the question, try to weed out the irrelevant information to hear what the interviewer is asking; one word in the question could make a big difference in your answer.

[2. Verify the Objectives]

You can bet that when a consultant has her first meeting with a client, she always asks about objectives and goals. What are the client's expectations, and are those expectations realistic? Even if the objective to your case seems obvious, there is always a possibility of an additional, underlying objective. So ask, "One objective is to raise profits. Are there any other objectives that I should know about?" If the interviewer says, "No. Higher profits is the only objective," then we can determine that the choice of case scenario comes directly from the objective. If there are two objectives, you will probably need to break the case in half and tackle one objective at a time.

At this point you should be able to determine whether this is a numbers case and should proceed accordingly. (Look back to page 18 for more information on numbers cases.)

[3. Ask Clarifying Questions]

As we've said, you ask questions for three reasons: to get additional information, to show the interviewer that you are not shy about asking questions, and to turn the case into a conversation. The key is to ask broad, open-ended questions that help you narrow the information at the start, because as the case progresses, you'll lose your "right" to ask these sweeping questions (it may give the impression that you're trying to get the interviewer to answer the case for you). The 11 case scenarios will guide you in asking these questions.

However, if you still don't know which scenario to use–i.e., whether this case is about increasing sales or increasing profits (or entering a new market, producing a new product, growing a company...) you can choose the appropriate case scenario by asking broad, generic questions about:

- the company : Is it public or private? How big is it? Is it growing?
- the industry : Where is the industry in its life cycle?
- competition : Both internal (Who are the major players? What is our market share?) and external market factors (i.e., substitutions, the economy, interest rates, unemployment rate, price-cutting by competitors, rising material costs).
- the product : If it's a new product, ask about both the advantages and the disadvantages. (Everyone forgets to ask about the disadvantages, but oftentimes disadvantages can drive your answer more than the advantages.)

*** Note :** *Keep in mind how the economy, the Internet, and other new technologies affect each question.*

[4. Lay Out Your Structure]

This is by far the toughest part of the process. You've decided which case scenario(s) to work with, and you have asked a few broad questions that have given you the information you need to form a logical response. Because you have studied the scenarios, you can quickly go through the bullet points in your mind and decide which are most relevant to this particular question. Then you just need to clue in the interviewer about how you plan to proceed.

With some cases, laying out your structure is the answer to the case itself–you tell the interviewer how you would go about fulfilling the company's objective, and voilà, you're done. With other cases, you'll actually need to walk through some of your proposed steps. It should be obvious (by the nature of the question and by the interviewer's feedback) which path a specific case calls for.

Many students find that it helps to draw a decision tree. A decision tree is a map of the reasoning process - visually breaking the case down into components and laying out your structure. It allows you to review your options and investigate the possible outcomes, while weighing the risks and rewards of each course of action.

*** Note** : *The more cases you practice, the more you'll be able to draw on those practice cases during the interview. For example, if you know you're working with an entering a new market case, you can think back to that Yellow Stuff Chemical Company case (page 90) and use it as a guide.*

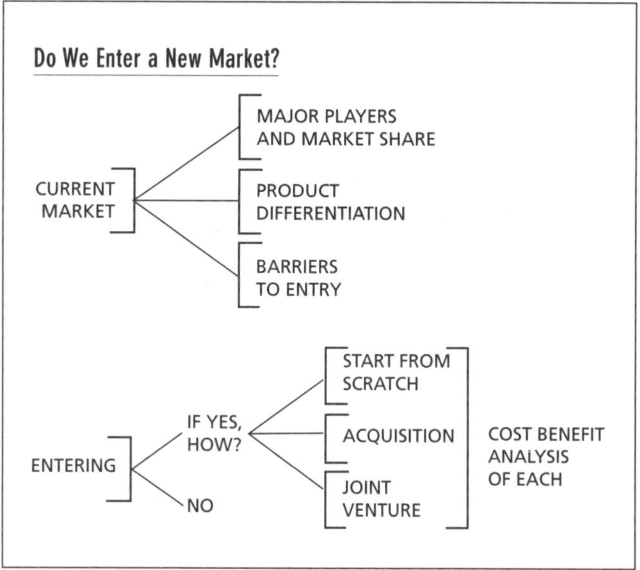

✛ The 11 Case Scenarios

[Entering a New Market]

Question : Your client manufactures hair products. It's thinking about entering the sunscreen market. Is this a good idea?

Step 1 : Investigate the market to determine whether entering the market would make good business sense.

- Who is our competition?
- What size market share does each competitor have?
- How do their products/services compare to ours?
- Are there any barriers to entry? Such as: capital requirements, access to distribution channels, proprietary product technology, or government policy.

Step 2 : If we decide to enter the market, we need to figure out the best way to become a player. There are three major ways to enter a new market:

- Start from scratch (see "Starting a New Business").
- Acquire an existing player within the desired industry.
- Form a joint venture/strategic alliance with another player with similar interests.

Analyze the pros and cons of each. This is sometimes called cost-benefit analysis. You can use this whenever you are trying to decide whether to proceed with a decision.

[Mergers and Acquisitions]

Question: Ben & Jerry's is buying a mid-size cream cheese manufacture. Does this make sense? What should they be thinking about?

Step 1: Determine the goals and objectives. Why are they buying it? Does it make good business sense, or are there better alternatives? Is it a good strategic move? Other reasons could be to:

- Increase market access
- Diversify their holdings
- Pre-empt the competition from getting it
- Gain tax advantages
- Incorporate synergies: marketing, financial, operations

Step 2: How much are they paying?

- Is the price fair?
- How are they going to pay for it?
- Can they afford it?
- If the economy sours, can they still make their debt payments?

Step 3: Due diligence, research the company and industry.

- What kind of shape is the company in?
- How secure are its markets and customers?
- How is the industry doing over all? And how is this company doing compared to the industry?
- How will our competitors respond to this acquisition?
- Are there any legal reasons why we can't, or shouldn't acquire it?

Step 4: Exit strategies

- How long are they planning on keeping it?
- Did they buy it to break it up and sell off parts of it?

[Developing a New Product]

Question : Our client has developed a new biodegradable product, which is both a soft drink and a car wax. What should they be thinking about?

You can approach the next four steps in any order you like.

Step 1 : Think about the product.

- What's special or proprietary about our product?
- Is the product patented?
- Are there similar products out there? Are there substitutions?
- What are the advantages and disadvantages of this new product?
- How does the new product fit in with the rest of our product line?

Step 2 : Think about our market strategy.

- How does this affect our existing product line?
- Are we cannibalizing one of our existing products?
- Are we replacing an existing product?
- How will this expand our customer base and increase our sales?
- What will the competitive response be?
- If it's a new market, what are the barriers to entering this market?
- Who are the major players and how much market share does each firm have?

Step 3 : Think about our customers.

- Who are our customers?
- How can we best reach them?
- Can we reach them through the Internet?
- How can we ensure that we retain them?

Step 4 : Think about financing.

- How is the project being funded?
- What is the best allocation of funds?
- Can we support the debt? (What if interest rates change? What if the economy sours?)

COST-DRIVEN PRICING
(The Deadly Business Sin)

Before there was Michael Porter and all the other modern day business gurus, there was Peter Drucker. The following is from Peter Drucker's ***Wall Street Journal*** article "The Five Deadly Business Sins."

The third deadly sin is cost-driven pricing. The only thing that works is price-driven costing. Most American and practically all European companies arrive at their prices by adding up costs and then putting a profit margin on top. And then as soon as they have introduced the product, they have to start cutting the price, have to redesign the product at enormous expense, have to take losses—and often, have to drop a perfectly good product because it is priced incorrectly. Their argument? "We have to recover our costs and make a profit."

This is true but irrelevant: Customers do not see it as their job to ensure manufacturers a profit. The only sound way to price is to start out with what the market is willing to pay—and thus, it must be assumed, what the competition will charge—and design to that price specification.

Cost-driven pricing is the reason there is no American consumer-electronics industry anymore. It had the technology and the products. But it operated on cost-led pricing —and the Japanese practiced price-led costing.[2]

[Pricing Strategies]

Question : Our client has developed a new Hollywood screenwriting software package.
How are we going to price it? What's our strategy and why?

Step 1 : Investigate the product.

- What's special or proprietary about our product?
- Are there similar products out there, and how are they priced?
- Where are we in the growth cycle of this industry? (Growth phase? Transition phase? Maturity phase?)
- How big is the market?
- What were our R&D costs?

Step 2 : Choose a pricing strategy.
Is the company in control of its own pricing strategies, or is it reacting to suppliers, the market, and its competitors?

- Cost-based pricing vs. price-based costing (i.e., do you decide pricing based on how much the product costs to produce or on how much people will pay?)
  - How much does it cost to make or deliver/provide?
  - What does the market expect to pay?
  - Is it a "must have" product?
  - Do we need to spend money to educate the consumer?
- Supply and demand (you'll win big points for graphing your answer)
  - What's the supply? How's the demand?
  - How will pricing have an affect on the market equilibrium?
  - Matching competition : What are similar products selling for?
  - Are there substitutions? (in this case, Microsoft Word, typewriters, etc.)

2 Peter Drucker. "The Five Deadly Business Sins." *The Wall Street Journal* (October 21, 1993).

[Growth Strategies]

Question : XYB Corporation has a high cash reserve (lots of cash on hand). How can we best use that money to grow the company?

Step 1 : Ask your feeler questions. Growth strategies could mean focusing on a certain product, division, or the company overall. This is a true strategic planning question, and you must determine the direction of questioning.

- Is the industry growing?
- How are we growing relative to the industry?
- Are our prices in line with our competitors?
- What have our competitors done in marketing and product development?
- Which segments of our business have the highest future potential?
- Do we have funding to support higher growth?

Step 2 : Choose a growth strategy. Increasing sales is one of the ways you grow, though not the only one. You need to determine if all or some of the following strategies for growth fit the question.

- Increase distribution channels.
- Increase product line.
- Invest in a major marketing campaign.
- Diversify products or services offered.
- Acquire competitors or a company in a different industry.

[Starting a New Business]

Question : Two brothers from Ireland want to start a travel magazine. They've come to us for strategic advice and to develop a business plan for getting started. What do you tell them?

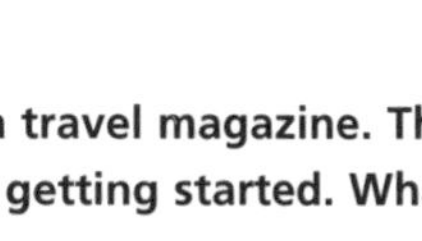

Step 1 : Starting a new business encompasses entering a new market as well–the first step is the same. Investigate the market to determine whether entering the market makes good business sense.

- Who is our competition?
- What size market share does each competitor have?
- How do their products/services compare to ours?
- Are there any barriers to entry? Such as: capital requirements, access to distribution channels, proprietary product technology, or government policy.

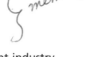

Step 2 : Once we determine that there are no barriers to entry, then we should look at the company from a venture capitalist point of view. Would you, as an outsider, invest in this start-up?

Would you risk your own money? Venture capitalists don't simply buy into an idea or product, they invest in the...

- Management
  - What is the management team like?
  - What are their core competencies?
  - Is there an advisory board?
- Market & Strategic Plan
  - What are the barriers to entering this market?
  - Who are the major players and what kind of market share does each firm have?
  - What will the competitive response be?
- Distribution Channels
  - What are our distribution channels?
- Product
  - What is the product and technology?
  - What is the competitive edge?
  - What are the disadvantages of this product?
  - Is the technology proprietary?
- Customers
  - Who are our customers?
  - How can we best reach them? Can we reach them on the Internet?
  - How can we ensure that we retain them?
- Finance
  - How is the project being funded?
  - What is the best allocation of funds?
  - Can we support the debt? (What if interest rates change? What if the economy sours?)

[Competitive Response]

Question : Sperry Topsider has developed a new non-slip sailing shoe that has been eating into the sales of our bestseller, the Commodore 2000. How can we respond?

Step 1 : If a competitor introduces a new product or picks up market share, we want to first ask such questions as:

- What is the competitor's new product and how does it differ from what we offer?
- What has the competitor done differently? What's changed?
- Have any other competitors picked up market share?

Step 2 : Choose one of the following response actions:

- Acquire the competitor, or another player in the same market.
- Merge with a competitor to create a strategic advantage and make us more powerful.
- Copy the competitor (e.g., Amazon.com vs. BarnesandNoble.com).

- Hire the competitor's top management.
- Increase our profile with a marketing and public relations campaign.

[Increasing Sales]

Question : BBB Electronics wants to increase its sales so it can claim that it is the largest distributor of the K6 double prong lightning rod. How can BBB Electronics reach its goal?

Step 1 : Increasing sales doesn't necessarily mean increasing profits. Think about the relationship. What can be done? What do we need to know?

- How are we growing relative to the industry?
- What has our market share done lately?
- Have we gone out and asked customers what they want from us?
- Are our prices in line with our competitors?
- What have our competitors done in marketing and product development?

Step 2 : There are four easy ways to increase sales. Determine which action (or combination thereof) is your best strategy:

- Increase volume. (Get more buyers, increase distribution channels, intensify marketing.)
- Increase amount of each sale. (Get each buyer to spend more.)
- Increase prices.
- Create seasonal balance. (Increase sales in every quarter–if you own a nursery, sell flowers in the spring, herbs in the summer, pumpkins in the fall, and trees and garlands in the winter.)

[Reducing Costs]

Question a : A publishing company is having a cash flow problem and needs to reduce its costs, otherwise it will have to layoff staff. How should the company proceed?

This is a straight reducing costs question. In such a scenario, you need to:

Step 1 : Ask for a breakdown of costs.
Step 2 : If any cost seems out of line, investigate why.
Step 3 : Benchmark the competitors.
Step 4 : Determine whether there are any labor-saving technologies that would help reduce costs.

Question b : EEC's sales are flat and profits are taking a header. How can we fix things?

If there has been a surge in costs, you need to approach this question by focusing on the internal and external costs that could account for the rise (e.g., If labor costs have skyrocketed, is it because of the good economy and because good workers are hard to find? Or is it that your workforce has unionized?) Examples of:

- Internal costs : union wages, suppliers, materials, economies of scale, increased support systems.
- External costs : economy, interest rates, government regulations, transportation/shipping strikes.

[Increasing the Bottom Line : Profits]

Question : Our client manufactures high-end athletic footwear. Sales are up, but profits are flat. What do we need to look at?

Whenever you hear the words "bottom line" or "profits" you should immediately think: Profits = (Revenues – Costs) x Volume. Because profits are an underlying theme in many cases, you need to make sure that profits is the main subject of the question before choosing to focus exclusively on this case scenario. (Asking feeler questions can help determine this–How have we been doing compared to the rest of the industry? How is the overall economy performing?) Price, costs and volume are all interdependent. You need to find the best mix, because changing one isn't always the best answer. If you cut prices to drive up volume, what happens to profit? Do profits increase or decrease? There needs to be a balance. The reason behind the decision needs to make sense.

Step 1 : Always look at the revenue ("price" is sometimes substituted) side first. Until you have identified your revenue streams, you can't know where best to cut costs.

- What are the revenue streams? (Where does the money come from?)
- What percentage of the total revenue does each stream represent?
- Does anything seem unusual in the balance of percentages?
- Have those percentages changed lately? If so, why?

Step 2 : Examine your costs.

- Identify the major variable and fixed costs.
- Have there been any major shifts in costs? (e.g., labor or raw material costs)
- Do any of these costs seem out of line?
- How can we reduce costs without damaging the revenue streams?
- Benchmark costs against our competitors.

Step 3 : Determine whether you want to pump up the volume. If so, you can:

- Expand into new areas.
- Increase sales force.
- Increase marketing.
- Reduce prices.
- Improve customer service.

[Turnarounds]

Question : AAS Company is in trouble and you've been brought in to save it. What do you do?

Step 1 : Gather information:

- Tell me about the company.
- Why is it failing? Bad products, bad management, bad economy?
- Tell me about the industry.
- Are our competitors facing the same problems?
- Do we have access to capital?
- Is it a public or privately held company?

Step 2 : Choose the appropriate actions from the following list. While this isn't an Rx for all troubled companies, these are some of the main points and actions you should be thinking about:

- Learn as much about the business and its operations as possible.
- Review services, products, and finances. (Are products out of date? Do we have a high debt load?)
- Secure sufficient financing so your plan has a chance.
- Review talent and temperament of all employees, and get rid of the deadwood.
- Determine short-term and long-term company goals.
- Devise a business plan.
- Visit clients, suppliers, and distributors, and reassure them.
- Prioritize goals and get some small successes under your belt ASAP to build confidence.

5 : Additional Tools & Frameworks

In this section, we will explore some supplements to the Ivy Case System. These include both other frameworks and additional tools so that you have an understanding of what else is out there. I've purposely limited the number of alternatives, however, because I've learned from experience that too many options can become a burden. Keep in mind that none of these frameworks or tools was specifically designed to answer case questions. It is far better to understand the underlying problems of the case and how to logically address those problems than to try to apply a "fix-all" framework. That being said...

✛ Five C's and Four P's

These are two elementary frameworks that can do the job. You're not going to blow anyone away with these, but you won't drown either. They will allow you to touch on all the main points and appear fairly well-organized.

There are two secrets to using these frameworks. First, since every case is different, the C's or the P's have to be rearranged to fit the case. If you treat these frameworks like a laundry list, your answer will seem nonlinear and possibly disorganized. Second, you need to kick up some dust to conceal the fact that you're using these frameworks. If your interviewer discovers you're using the Five C's or Four P's you might lose some points; neither of these frameworks is particularly impressive.

[Five C's]

- **Company :** What do you know about the company? How big is it? Is it a public or private company? What kinds of products or services does it offer to its clients?
- **Costs :** What are the major costs? How have its costs changed in the past year? How do its costs compare to others in the industry? How can we reduce costs?
- **Competition :** Who are the biggest competitors? What market share does each player hold? Has market share changed in the last year? How do our services or products differ from the competition? Do we hold any strategic advantage over our competitors?
- **Consumer :** Consumers/clients. Who are they? What do they want? Are we fulfilling their needs? How can we get more? Are we keeping the ones we have?

[Four P's]

- **Product :** What are our products and services? What is the company's niche?
- **Price :** How does our price compare to the competitors'? How was our price determined? Are we priced right? If we change our price, what will that do to our sales volume?
- **Place :** How do we get our products to the end user? How can we increase our distribution channels? Do our competitors have products in places that we don't? Do they serve markets that we can't reach? If so, why? And how can we reach them?
- **Promotions :** How can we best market our product? Are we reaching the right

- **Channels :** Distribution channels. How do we get our product into the hands of the end users? How can we increase our distribution channels? Are there areas of our market that we are not reaching? How do we reach them?

market? What kind of marketing campaigns has the company done in the past? Were they effective? Can we afford to increase our marketing campaign?

+ BCG Matrix

In 1998, Wiley Press published Perspectives on Strategy. The book is a collection of articles and essays written by senior members of The Boston Consulting Group. One popular and useful framework is the BCG "Product Portfolio Matrix." This matrix is designed to place a product or group of products into one of four categories while taking into account a company's relative market share. BCG has been kind enough to let us reprint Chapter Three.

The Product Portfolio
(*Bruce D. Henderson, 1970*)[3]

To be successful, a company should have a portfolio of products with different growth rates and different market shares. The portfolio composition is a function of the balance between cash flows. High-growth products require cash inputs to grow. Low-growth products should generate excess cash. Both kinds are needed simultaneously.

Four rules determine the cash flow of a product.

- Margins and cash generated are a function of market share. High margins and high market share go together. This is a matter of common observation, explained by the experience curve effect.

- Growth requires cash input to finance added assets. The added cash required to hold share is a function of growth rates.

- High market share must be earned or bought. Buying market share requires an additional increment of investment.

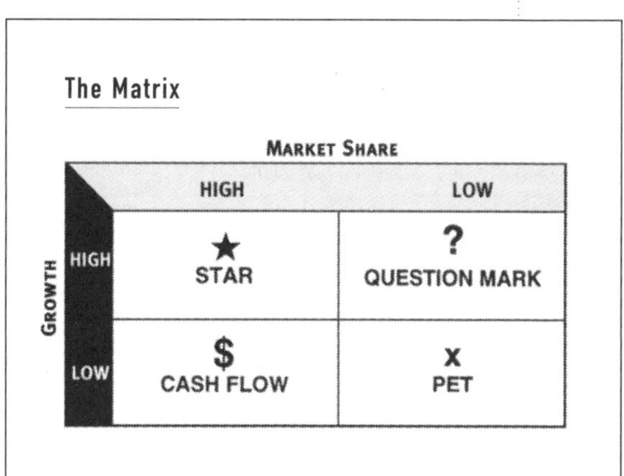

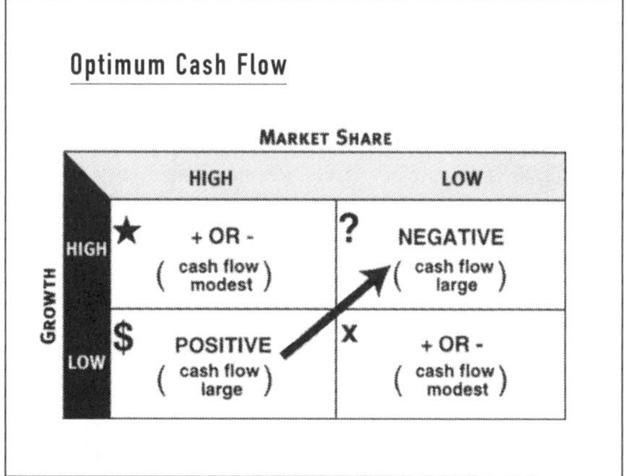

3 Used with permission of The Boston Consulting Group. Bruce D. Henderson, "The Product Portfolio," *Perspectives on Strategy from The Boston Consulting Group*, ed. Carl W. Stern and George Stalk, Jr. (New York: John Wiley & Sons, Inc., 1998), pp.35–37.

• No product market can grow indefinitely. The payoff from growth must come when the growth slows, or it never will. The payoff is cash that cannot be reinvested in that product.

Products with high market share and slow growth are cash cows. Characteristically, they generate large amounts of cash, in excess of the reinvestment required to maintain share. This excess need not, and should not, be reinvested in those products. In fact, if the rate of return exceeds the growth rate, the cash cannot be reinvested indefinitely, except by depressing returns.

Products with low market share and low growth are pets. They may show an accounting profit, but the profit must be reinvested to maintain share, leaving no cash throw-off. The product is essentially worthless, except in liquidation.

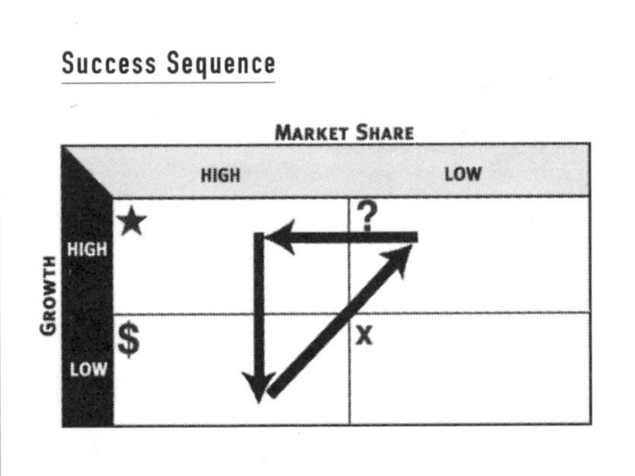

Disaster Sequence

Market Share

High | Low

Growth: High / Low

★ ? $ X

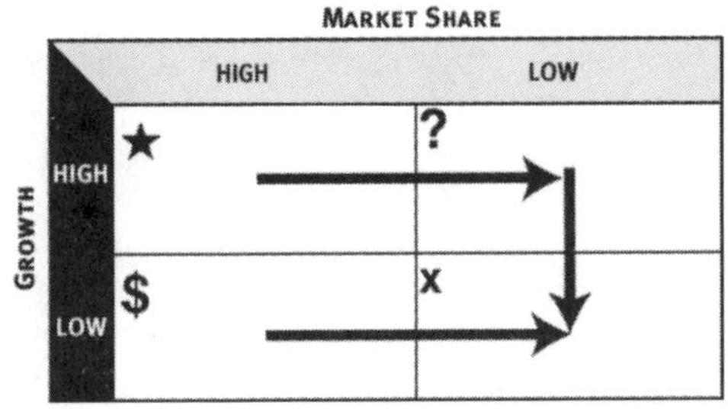

All products eventually become either cash cows or pets. The value of a product is completely dependent upon obtaining a leading share of its market before the growth slows.

Low-market-share, high-growth products are the question marks. They almost always require far more cash than they can generate. If cash is not supplied, they fall behind and die. Even when the cash is supplied, if they only hold their share, they are still pets when the growth stops. The question marks require large added cash investments for market share to be purchased. The low-market-share, high-growth product is a liability unless it becomes a leader. It requires very large cash inputs that it cannot generate itself.

The high-share, high-growth product is the star. It nearly always shows reported profits, but it may or may not generate all of its own cash. If it stays a leader, however, it will become a large cash generator when growth slows and its reinvestment requirements diminish. The star eventually becomes the cash cow, providing high volume, high margin, high stability, security, and cash throw-off for reinvestment elsewhere.

The payoff for leadership is very high indeed if it is achieved early and maintained until growth slows. Investment in market share during the growth phase can be very attractive if you have the cash. Growth in market is compounded by growth in share. Increases in share increase the margin. High margin permits higher leverage with equal safety. The resulting profitability permits higher payment of earnings after financing normal growth. The return on investment is enormous.

The need for a portfolio of businesses becomes obvious. Every company needs products in which to invest cash. Every company needs products that generate cash. And every product should eventually be a cash generator; otherwise it is worthless.

Only a diversified company with a balanced portfolio can use its strengths to truly capitalize on its growth opportunities. The balanced portfolio has:

- stars whose high share and high growth assure the future
- cash cows that supply funds for that high growth
- question marks to be converted into stars with the added funds

Pets are not necessary. They are evidence of failure either to obtain a leadership position during the growth phase or to get out and cut the losses.

+ Michael Porter's "Five Forces" / The Structural Analysis of Industries

Michael Porter didn't develop his "Five Forces" as a case framework. However, when you are given a case dealing with developing a new product, entering a new market, or starting a new business, this framework works quite well (e.g., A regional food manufacturer is thinking of entering the gourmet toothpaste business. Should the company take the plunge?)

Please refer to Michael Porter's bestseller, *Competitive Strategy*, for a more in-depth explanation of his "Five Forces" model.

Porter writes that the state of competition in an industry depends on five basic competitive forces:

1. The threat of new or potential entrants. This includes new companies or acquisitions of established companies by a new player. If barriers are high or if newcomers can expect entrenchment or retaliatory measures from existing competitors, such as a price war, then the threat of entry is low. According to Porter, barriers of entry include:

- economies of scale
- capital requirements
- government policy
- switching costs
- access to distribution channels
- product differentiation
- proprietary product technology

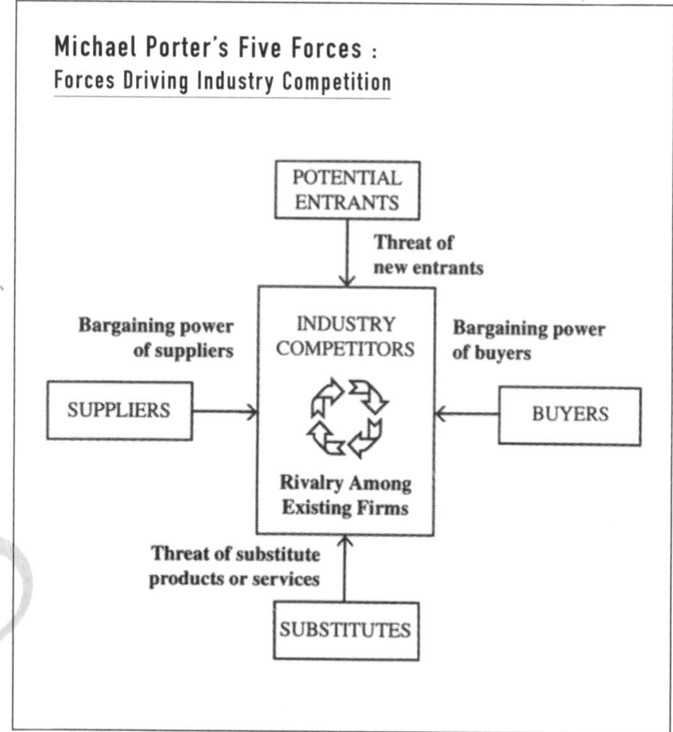

2. Intensity of rivalry among existing competitors.
3. Pressure from substitution products, e.g., sugar vs. high-fructose corn syrup and artificial sweeteners.
4. Bargaining power of buyers. Buyers compete with the industry by forcing down prices, bargaining for higher quality or more services, and playing competitors against each other–all at the expense of industry profitability.
5. Bargaining power of suppliers. Forces 4 and 5 have to do with supply and demand. When there are many suppliers but few buyers, the buyers have the upper hand. When there are many buyers, but few suppliers, the suppliers have the advantage.

+ Income Statement

While you may never have to draw up an income statement, you may be handed one in an interview and be asked to analyze it. Understanding the basics of an income statement is essential for answering product and company profitability questions. How do the costs stack up? Do any numbers seem out of line or a bit high? For example, if Joe's Shoe Company's labor costs were $50,000 instead of $15,000, that should send off warning bells that something is wrong. Why are labor costs $50,000, or 50% of gross revenues?

Joe's Shoe Company
Income Statement

	Gross Revenues (units times price)		**100,000**
(–)	Returns & discounts	(5,000)	
	Net Sales		**95,000**
(–)	Cost of Goods Sold		
	Direct Labor	(15,000)	
	Direct Material Costs	(10,000)	
	Overhead	(5,000)	
	Delivery Costs	(5,000)	
		(35,000)	
	Gross Margin		**60,000**
(–)	Selling, General & Admin.	(20,000)	
(–)	Depreciation	(5,000)	
		(25,000)	
	Operating Profits		**35,000**
(–)	Interest Expense	(3,000)	
	Profit Before Taxes		**32,000**

✛ "If" Scenarios to Remember

Sales Scenarios

- If sales are flat and profits are taking a header, you need to examine both revenues and costs. Always start with the revenue side first. Until you identify and understand the revenue streams, you can't make educated decisions on the cost side.
- If sales are flat but market share remains relatively constant, that could indicate that industry sales are flat and that your competitors are experiencing similar problems.
- If your case includes a decline-in-sales problem, analyze these three things:
  - Overall declining market demand (e.g., soda sales have dropped as bottled water becomes the drink of choice).
  - The current marketplace might be mature or your product may be obsolete (e.g., vinyl records give way to CDs).
  - Loss of market share due to substitutions (e.g., video rentals have declined because there are numerous substitutions vying for the leisure dollar, such as going out to dinner, going to the movies, pay-per-view, direct TV, and the Internet).
- If sales and market share are increasing, but profits are declining, then you need to investigate whether prices are dropping and/or costs are climbing. However, if costs aren't the issue, then investigate product mix, and check to see if the margins have changed.

Profit Scenarios

- If profits are declining because of a drop in revenues, concentrate on marketing and distribution issues.
- If profits are declining because of rising expenses, concentrate on operational and financial issues, i.e., COGS (cost of goods sold), labor, rent, and marketing costs.
- If profits are declining, yet revenues went up, review:
  - Changes in costs
  - Any additional expenses
  - Changes in prices
  - The product mix
  - Changes in customers' needs

Product Scenarios

- If a product is in its emerging growth stage, concentrate on R&D, competition, and pricing.
- If a product is in its growth stage, emphasize marketing and competition.
- If a product is in its mature stage, focus on manufacturing, costs, and competition.
- If a product is in its declining stage, define niche market, analyze the competition's play, or think exit strategy.

Pricing Scenarios

If you lower prices, and volume rises and you are pushed beyond full capacity, then your costs will shoot up as your employees work overtime, and consequently your profits will suffer.

Prices are stable only when three conditions are met:[3]

- Growth rate for all competitors is approximately the same.
- Prices are paralleling costs.
- Prices of all competitors are roughly of equal value.

The volume (the amount that you produce) and the costs are easier to change than the industry price levels, unless everyone changes their prices together (e.g., airline tickets or gas prices).

The perfect strategy for the high-cost producer is one that convinces competitors that market shares cannot be shifted, except over long periods of time, and therefore, that the highest practical industry prices are to everyone's advantage[4]–meaning that price wars are detrimental and everyone will profit more by keeping prices high.

General tips

- How the Internet affects the company should be in the back of your mind in every case.
- How the economy affects the company should be in the back of your mind in every case.
- How the competition, both internal to the industry and external (substitutions), affects the company should be in the back of your mind in every case.

+ Business Case Tips

• This is more of a story than a tip. A student of mine studied hard for his case question interview, however, when the time came he froze. He just couldn't think how to begin. So he looked at the interviewer and said, "To be honest with you, I've already heard this question and feel that it wouldn't be fair for me to answer it." The interviewer thanked him for his honesty, then gave him another question which he easily nailed.

• Take graph paper into the interview. It helps you organize your thoughts, keeps the numbers lined up when you multiply and add, and reminds you to try to graph part of your answer.

• Ask for numbers. If the numbers aren't an important part of the case they will more than likely tell you not to focus on them.

• Practice your math, particularly multiplication and percentages. Almost all recruiters **will not** let you take a calculator into the interview. Most students make math mistakes. They are usually off by a zero or two.

• Interact with the interviewer as much as possible. Remember, it should be a conversation.

A final word before you tackle the cases.

---

3 Bruce D. Henderson, "The Product Portfolio," *Perspectives on Strategy from the Boston Consulting Group*, ed. Carl W. Stern and George Stalk, Jr. (New York: John Wiley & Sons, Inc., 1998), pp. 21.

4 Ibid., pp.27.

+ An Aristotelian Framework

Aristotle's book *Rhethoric and Poetics* was really the first case question interview prep book. His book is about persuasion and after all isn't that what we're trying to do — persuade the interviewer that we have what it takes. Aristotle lays out a tripod (a framework) and argues that persuasion relies on the relationship between logos, ethos and pathos. As you probably remember from Philosophy 101 logos is a logical, well-reasoned argument based on facts and figures, charts and graphs. Ethos deals with the speaker's (that's you) personal voice and character. How likeable and believable are you? In other words, fit. How would I feel if we were snowed in for nine hours at the Macedonian Chariot station? Would you be an interesting companion? Finally there is pathos, your audience's frame of mind. This is often tough to determine or control, but it can be massaged by incorporating logos and ethos into your answer. The point is that you need the tripod, the combination of logos, ethos and pathos to do well in a case interview. Too much logic and not enough personality results in a tipped tripod. As you prepare for your interviews remember to concentrate on all three. It is as much about the presentation as it is about the logic.

✣ A Case of Bud

◗ Case 1 : Our client is Anheuser Busch. Their flagship product is Budweiser. They want to know if they should switch Budweiser from glass to plastic bottles. What are the advantages and disadvantages of such a move? And estimate for me the size of the U.S. beer market.

What's Budweiser's objective?

– To increase profits and market share.

What kind of market share does Budweiser have?

– Anheuser Busch and its thirty products have 46 percent of the domestic market. Bud and Bud Light make up 20 percent of the market.

Is that 20 percent of the 46 percent or 20 percent of the overall market?

– It's 20 percent of the overall market.

Let's first take a minute to figure out the size of the U.S. beer market. I'd like to break it down by generation. I'll assume that there are 280 million Americans. I'll also assume that there are even numbers of people in each generation. So there are 70 million people per generation.

- **I'll estimate that the people in generation one, the 0 to 20 year olds will not drink.**
- **The second generation, the 21 to 40 year-olds are probably the heaviest beer drinkers. I'll assume that 75 percent of them drink beer and that they have 5 beers a week or 250 beers a year. So that is 52.5 or 52 million drinkers times 250 beers equals 13 billion beers.**
- **The folks in the third generation – I estimate that 50 percent of them drink beer and that they have 3 beers a week or 150 beers a year. So that will equal 5.2 billion beers.**
- **The last generation, or as Tom Brokaw calls the greatest generation - I'll assume that only 20 percent of them drink beer, so that's 14 million, and that they drink two beers a week or 1.4 billion beers a year.**

Age	# of People (in millions)	% that drink beer	# of beer drinkers	# of beers per week	# of beers per year (50 weeks)	Approximate totals
0-20	70	0	0	0	0	0
21-40	70	75%	52.5 million	5	250	13 billion
41-60	70	50%	35 million	3	150	5.2 billion
61-80	70	20%	14 million	2	100	1.4 billion
Totals	280					19.6 or 20 billion

These totals include drinking beer at home and drinking beer in public, like bars and restaurants. The total is 19.6 or 20 billion beers.

Now do you want this in a dollar amount or calculated by the bottle?

– By the bottle.

Well we came up with 20 billion beers. I'll assume that bottles and cans sell the same so we'll assume a 50/50 split – cans to bottles. So that means we are talking 10 billion bottles of beer. Now you mentioned that Bud and Bud Light make up 20 percent of that market so we're looking at 20 percent of 10 billion, which is 2 billion bottles of Bud, and Bud Light sold each year.

– Okay, good. Let's move on to the rest of the question.

I have a few questions. Does plastic have the same shelf life as glass and aluminum?

– Yes, if the bottle is brown.

Does the plastic bottle stay as cold as glass and aluminum?

– It stays as cold as long as glass, colder and longer than aluminum.

Does the bottle affect the taste?

– No.

Have any of our competitors switched to plastic bottles?

– Assume no.

I assume that the weight of plastic is about half of what glass is.

– Actually plastic weighs one-seventh of what glass weighs.

So it is lighter, which will save on shipping costs. Is it cheaper?

– Yes. It's about half the price. Assume that it costs Bud 6 cents for each glass bottle and 3 cents for each plastic bottle.

Do they have to retool the plant?

– Good question. There will be some modifications. Beer is boiling hot when it is bottled. So between the heat and the pressure in which the beer is forced into the bottles, unless the beer is cooled first, the plastic bottle could get disfigured. In addition, the capping system is different. Plastic will have screw on caps.

What is the expected cost of retooling the plant?

– Ten million dollars.

Do they expect to sell more Bud because it's in a plastic bottle?

– What do you think?

I think that there is an emotional bond between beer drinkers and glass. I'd like to go back and find out what the industry did to introduce the metal cans.

That's a good idea, but we don't have that info right now.

Well, first I think that if you switched completely from glass to plastic you would lose the loyal middle-aged beer drinker. I would just offer it as a packaging option. People could buy

plastic if they wanted to, but they could still get glass. I'd try to test market it for eighteen months in six cosmopolitan cities. I'd also gear my advertising toward the young adults, people who are in their twenties and thirties who grew up drinking soda out of a plastic bottle. I'd also mimic the soda in the sense that I would package the beer in 12 ounce and 20 ounce "Tall Boy" bottles. That way you'd sell more beer. In addition, you said that the plastic bottle would have screw-on caps. This makes great sense with a 20 ounce bottle.

The other huge market I see is the sports stadium. It's probably safer for everyone if beer was sold in plastic bottles during baseball, basketball, football and certainly hockey games. Plastic would also be perfect for taking beer to the beach or around a pool. Oh, I almost forgot, there would be less breakage, both while drinking and shipping the product.

– What are the economics of this decision?

We came up with 2 billion bottles of Bud sold each year. The price of a plastic bottle is three cents less. So 3 cents times 2 billion equals 60 million which is significantly more than the 10 million it will cost us to retool the plant. Add in the money we will save on shipping cost and less breakage. So economically it makes sense to at least test market it.

– Okay, good. So summarize for me. What are the advantages and disadvantages? And what would you tell Bud to do?

I would tell Bud that they should test market the plastic bottle and maybe have it as a packaging option. I would also tell them that I would never get rid of the glass bottle. There is too much history there. They would certainly lose market share. They may even want to try it out first in one of their lesser brands.

Since the objective is to increase profits, I'd like to break the advantages down in two ways, reductions in costs and increases in revenues. Let's start with the savings in costs. One, plastic is cheaper than glass. So we would save money in the manufacturing, because the fixed cost would go down. Two, our shipping costs would be less because plastic weighs one-seventh of what glass weighs. In addition there would be less breakage during shipping. We would be able to increase sales because we could sell the beer in larger sized bottles. We might even be able to increase our market share with beer drinkers between the ages of twenty-one and thirty nine.

The disadvantages might be image. After all we are the "King of Beers." But if we offer it as a packaging option then the traditionalists might not care. The other disadvantage might be that if we produce beer in plastic bottles younger drinkers might gulp beer as they do soda. This could cause more drunk driving accidents. We would need to keep a close eye on that.

Good job.

- **Type of Case: Strategy / market-sizing / cost benefit analysis**
- **Comments: Good analysis of both the economic and emotional issues needed to make this decision. Also, unlike most people I gave this case to, her decision wasn't an either or, she came up with the packaging option strategy despite the favorable economic pressures.**

Rock n Roll Suicide

Case 2 : You are a concert promoter in a mid-Western city. You have a chance to book David Bowie in the city-owned Forum. The Forum holds 8,100 fans. (Assume that 100 tickets will been given away as promotional tickets). David Bowie wants $350,000 to appear. Do you book him?

Does it make good business sense to book David Bowie in the Forum? Besides making money, are their any other objectives I should take into consideration?

– No.

Do we know what tickets will sell for?

– You're the promoter. I can tell you that, in New York, David Bowie sold out a venue that held 20,000 fans with an average ticket price of $100 dollars. In Boston he sold out a 15,000 fan venue with an average ticket price of $85, but that was in slightly better economic times.

As a starting point I'll divide 350,000 by 8,000 and we get ... around $45 per ticket. I know that there are a number of other expenses as well. Besides the cost of the talent there are marketing and promotion costs, venue rental, security - that sort of thing.

– Assume that security comes with the venue rental. I can tell you that the Forum rents for $100,000. That includes a day of setup and rehearsal and the concert date.

So 350,000 for the talent, 100,000 for the venue and let's say 50,000 for marketing and promotion. That brings our total costs to $500,000.

Costs

- **Talent - $350,000**
- **Marketing and promotion - $50,000**
- **Venue rental and insurance- $100,000**

Total Costs - $500,000

Okay, then 500,000 divided by 8000 equals around $63. Can I assume that Bowie will sell out the Forum?

– I don't think that that's a fair assumption. I can tell you that there is a relationship between the price of the ticket and how many seats you'll sell. In fact we've done a study. If the ticket price is $40 there is a 100% chance of a sellout. If the tickets average $60 there is a 90% of a sellout. An average ticket price of $75 will bring a 75% chance of a sellout, while an $85 ticket average will most likely only sell 65% of the tickets. If you try to price the tickets at $100 then you'll only fill half the Forum.

Before I look at the other revenue streams I'd like calculate the ticket revenues. I'm going to take a second to make a chart.

No. of Seats	Average Price/ticket	Chance of a sellout	Tickets sold	Ticket Revenue
8,000	$40	100%	8,000	$320,000
8,000	$60	90%	7,200	$432,000
8,000	$75	75%	6,000	$450,000
8,000	$85	65%	5,200	$442,000
8,000	$100	50%	4,000	$400,000

Based solely on ticket sales we see that we'll bring in the most revenue if we sell the tickets for an average price of $75. That will bring in $450,000. However, I'll assume that there are other revenue streams. I'm not sure how these work, but I'd expect that we get a cut of the parking, concessions and merchandise.

– I can help you there. You get 50 percent of the concession sales, 50% of the parking, and 25% of the merchandising.

We get 100 percent of the ticket sales averaging $75. You said we get 50% of the concession sales. I'd think that people would spend on average around $20 each. That means 8,000 times $20 divided by 2 equals 8,000 times 10 or $80,000.

Parking, I'm going to assume that _ of the patrons drive and park in our facility and that parking is $20 per car. That's 2,000 cars. We get 50% so that's 20,000.

Merchandise, not everyone buys merchandise because it tends to be fairly expensive. Other fans buy a ton of stuff. I'll assume that on average people spend $24. Let's calculate 8,000 times 24 divided by 4 or 8,000 times $6 which equals $48,000.

Revenues

- **Ticket sales -**
- **Concession sales - you get 50% (avg. $20/ person)**
- **Parking – you get 50% (1/4 of seats sold – parking is $20 a car)**
- **Merchandise – you get 25% (avg. $24 person)**

– Yes, but you just said that you'd go with the $75 ticket average which means that there will only be 6,000 fans, not 8,000 that you are doing your calculations on.

Yes, well I'm just filling out the rest of the chart. I'll do the same for each ticket price.

	$40 a ticket	$60	$75	$85	$100
Ticket Sales	320,000	432,000	450,000	442,000	400,000
Concessions	80,000	72,000	60,000	52,000	40,000
Parking	20,000	18,000	15,000	13,000	10,000
Merchandise	48,000	43,200	36,000	31,200	24,000
Total	468,000	565,200	561,000	538,200	474,000

If my extended chart is correct, then I'd switch to a $60 ticket average where revenues would be $565,200 versus $561,000 for the $75 ticket. The difference is $4,200.

I would go ahead and book him because our total revenues would be $565,200 and our total costs would be $500,000 leaving a profit of $65,200.

– That's it? That's your answer?

Ah, yes.

– Isn't there anything else you'd like to know or say?

I can get you a couple back-stage passes.

– First off your answers are off by $1850. (off the student's look) You forgot to add in the 100 promotional tickets. Chances are that they will park, eat and buy merchandise.

What if I told you that Bowie would do two shows for a total of $500,000? How does that change your answer?

It would lower some of my costs. Besides the cost of talent, the marketing and promotion cost could be spread over both concerts. How about the cost of the venue? Do we get a discount for a two-night booking?

– No.

So our new costs for the two night concert are:

Costs
- **Talent - $500,000**
- **Marketing and promotion - $50,000**
- **Venue rental and insurance- $200,000**

Total Costs - $750,000

What about our predictions of a sell out?

– If the ticket price is $40 there is a 100% chance of a sellout on both nights. If the tickets average $60 there is a 75% of a sellout on both nights. An average ticket price of $75, $85 or $100 will bring a 50% chance you'll only fill half the Forum.

Let me take a moment to do the calculations. I'll assume that all the percentages of the revenue streams remain the same.

No. of Seats	Average Price/ticket	Chance of a sellout	Tickets sold	Ticket Revenue
16,000	$40	100%	16,000	$640,000
16,000	$60	75%	12,000	$720,000

As far as ticket revenues go we would earn more with the $60 ticket. About $80,000 more, that's pretty significant. It looks like we'll go with the $60 ticket; let me calculate the other revenues.

	$40 a ticket	$60 a ticket
Ticket Sales	640,000	720,000
Concession Sales	160,000	120,000
Parking	40,000	30,000
Merchandise	96,000	72,000
Total Revenues	936,000	942,000

It's a lot closer than I would have figured. There's only a $6,000 difference.

– So what are you going to do?

It's a no-brainer. I'd go with the $40 tickets and the right to boast that we sold out two shows. In addition, I think that it will make David Bowie happier that he sold out and that the ticket prices were low enough so that everyone who wanted to see the show could afford to go.

– Anything else?

Yes, you'll still get your back-stage passes.

– What if you went with the $60 ticket then gave away the remaining ticket so you can collect the additional revenues from the extra parking, concessions and merchandising sales?

That would work too.

– Thanks for coming in. Next.

Type of Case: Pricing

Comments: She did a decent job. The interviewer caught her in a mistake or two, but she was able to recover pretty quickly. She lost points for not asking or investigating the possibility of doing two shows. Her math was good and she was well organized using charts. She gained a few points for picking the $40 tickets over the $60 tickets even though it was less money.

+ House of Pizza

Case 3 : A major video store chain is considering the acquisition of a national chain of pizza restaurants. What factors are important in making this decision?

So you have a major video store chain, I'm assuming like Blockbuster or Hollywood, who is considering purchasing a national chain of pizza restaurants. They want to know what they should be looking at in order to make this decision. Why are they doing this? What are their main objectives?

– Why do you think?

Could be a number of things. Profit, increased market access, to pre-empt the competition from buying into the pizza market and financial, operational and marketing synergies.

– Say all of the above.

How many restaurants are there in the chain?

– Six hundred.

Where are they located?

– Mostly in, and around the major cities.

Does the pizza chain currently own all its stores, or do they franchise?

– They own all their stores.

Who are the major players and what size market share does each have? What size market share do we have?

– Pizza Hut has 46 percent of the market, Domino's 21 percent, Little Caesar's 13 percent, Papa John's has 5 percent and we have 3 percent. All the others – the little guys make up the remaining 12 percent.

Is there anything else you can tell me about the pizza market?

– Sure, what do you want to know? I can tell you that Americans eat 350 slices of pizza per second. That pizza is a $33 billion per year industry. That pizzerias represent approximately 20 percent of all restaurants in the United States and that 93 percent of Americans eat at least one slice of pizza per month. And, oh, pizza restaurant growth continues to out pace overall restaurant growth. You find any of that helpful?

Well, yes, particularly the last part about its growth.

– Why? What does that tell you?

That it is, and continues to be a very competitive market. You asked me about major factors. The first factor is the market. If the company that we want to buy has 3 percent of a $33 billion dollar industry that means our sales must be about $100 million.

– What? Three percent of 33 billion is 100,000 million? Try again.

I mean a billion. I was off by a zero. So, if we are serious about entering the pizza industry then I think buying our way in is the only way to go. With all the competition it would be very difficult to differentiate ourselves, it would take a long time to build brand, find great locations, build-out the restaurants, and put together a management and sales team.

– And that's why we're buying our way in. Tell me something new.

We have been running a retail business, so this isn't something entirely new. We're going after the same market. I think that there could be a lot of synergies, a lot of crossover promotions. We might even combine some of the stores. Build ones that sell pizzas and rent DVDs. People could order their pizza, pick out a DVD and by that time the pizza would be ready.

– Good. Anything else?

Do we have the cash or would we have to finance this acquisition?

– We are financing about half. What makes you think we can do a better job at running the pizza chain?

We might be able to look at the business more objectively. We can visit the idea of franchising. We can visit the idea of spinning this division off in an IPO once the market rebounds. Is this chain profitable? If so, what were the profits over the last five years?

– After tax profits have been falling over the last five years. Five years ago the company made $100 million on $500 million in sales. This year we made $30 million on $1billion in sales.

So they've gone from a 20 percent return to a 3 percent return. Have you done an analysis on why the sales are dropping?

– I didn't say the sales are dropping. I said that after tax profits were dropping.

Sorry, that's what I meant.

What do you think is happening?

I'll assume that the reason our sales have doubled over the last five years is because we are opening up new stores. We have invested heavily in this growth. It's time to take a close look at all the stores and find out which ones are profitable and which ones aren't. I'd analyze the ones that aren't, try to fix them and if they can't be turned around in six months we might want to consider closing them.

What else?

Next, I'd ask for a breakdown of our costs. How fast have they been climbing? I'd look to see if there any costs that are out of line. Maybe we're paying too much for space? Maybe our labor costs have skyrocketed? Are there any laborsaving technologies that would reduce

costs? I'd see where we could cut back without jeopardizing the quality of the product. I'd also benchmark our costs against our competitors.

– All right. I'm feeling a little better about you, but I have to tell you your answer was all over the place. If you give me a great summary, I might call you back.

Pizza is a growth industry. It's a very large and extremely competitive market. It makes sense to enter it if we are convinced that we can increase the company's profits. First, we need to look at revenue streams. What can we be doing that we're not? How can we increase sales? What percentage does each of the revenue streams represent? Does anything seem unusual in the balance of percentages? Have percentages changed lately? If so, why?

We also need to take a close look at costs. What's out of line? What can be reduced through technology? Have there been any major shifts in costs – like labor or raw materials? And how can we streamline work processes to reduce costs.

Next, I'd do a store analysis. Get rid of the dogs, while looking for new locations. The other component in the profit formula is volume. How do we jack-up volume? One way is to open more stores. Another is to increase our marketing efforts, and a third is to reduce prices to drive in traffic. And finally, improve customer service so the customers that do come in, come back.

– So getting back to the original question.

What factors are important in making this decision? Is the price of the company reasonable? Can we afford it and service the debt when the economy is down? Is the brand strong? Can we reasonably expect to build on that brand? Do we have the expertise to increase sales while reducing costs? Are there synergies that would benefit both companies? And finally, we need to consider the post acquisition integration issues. Things like cultural implications, strategic fit and possible exit strategies.

– That's it? That's the best you can do?

Given the time we have, yes. Give me more time and access to resources and I can do better.

Thanks.

Type of Case: Combination of acquisition, entering a new market and improving the bottom line.

Comments: The student was strong in the beginning, and then he lost his way. He seemed to get pushed around by the interviewer. However, he did come on strong at the end with an articulate summary.

+ Eastern Training Network

Case 4 : Our client is a mid-size training company that serves New England and the Atlantic Seaboard regions. They offer a variety of computer training and consulting services. Eastern just found out that IBM is going to enter into their segment of the market. What do they do?

Eastern Training Network just found out that IBM is entering their segment of the market and wants to know what to do. I'm assuming that the objectives are to either keep IBM out of our market or to maintain as much market share as we can. Is that a fair set of assumptions?

– Yes.

Are there any other objectives that I should be aware of?

– No.

Are there other firms in our area that we currently compete with?

– Yes. Including us, there are three major players that do what we do and maybe three smaller firms that serve one or two clients exclusively.

Do we know what Eastern's market share is?

– Eastern's market share within the region is 24 percent.

Do we know what our two other competitors are doing to keep IBM out?

– No. Good question but not relevant.

Since one of my major objectives is to maintain market share I'd break my strategy down into three prongs. First, I'd try to keep IBM out. Second, I'd try to protect what's mine. And third I'd go after new customers.

– Explain.

I would try to figure out what I can do to raise the barriers of entry and keep IBM out. Since they have almost unlimited resources and because this is an unregulated industry I think the chances of that are pretty nil.

Second, I'd try to protect what's mine. It is much cheaper to keep your current customers than it is to go out and get new ones. So I'd do three things. I'd raise switching costs. Make it so that it wouldn't make sense to leave us for IBM.

– Give me an example.

Well since I don't know the industry that well I'd like to give another example. AOL makes it hard for customers to leave because they have what are called "sticky" features. Customers have their email address with AOL, they have their address book with AOL, and their customers have access to certain web information and additional benefits. So to switch over to another Internet provider becomes a hassle.

– Point taken. What's next?

I'd protect what's mine. I'd visit with my customers and find out what is important to them. Maybe increase my promotional efforts. Maybe come up with customer loyalty programs. Make them feel wanted and special. Everyone likes to feel appreciated. And third, I would do everything I could to establish long-term contracts to lock customers in. To go along with that I'd build in incentives or give commissions to our sales staff to resign a client.

– Third?

Bring in new customers. I'd increase my marketing efforts, place ads, go to conventions, lobby for state contracts. I'd try to steal sales staff and customers away from my competition. And finally I would grow through acquisition. You mentioned that there were a number of smaller players that had one or two big accounts. I'd see if they would like to sell their businesses.

– Don't you think that's risky? To lay out capital to buy up small firms when IBM is coming to town. What's to guarantee that the small firm's clients won't jump to IBM?

There are no guarantees. However, being IBM is a double-edged sword. On one hand IBM is big, has an incredible amount of resources and they have the potential to do great things. On the other hand, it is because they are so big that things might very well fall through the cracks. Am I wrong in thinking that the training we offer is similar to what IBM offers? I think the things that will differentiate us are our people and our customer service. We're going to fight and do everything we can to hold on to our customer base while we prospect for new business. Being the biggest isn't always an advantage.

– What if IBM comes in and offers the same services you do, but offers a steep discount for clients to sign up? Do you lower your prices?

No. I wouldn't engage in a price war with IBM. There is no way to win. I believe that Eastern offers great products at competitive prices. If customers like us they're not going to go to IBM to save a little money. This is not like shopping around for the best deal on a new refrigerator. We're in the services business; it's all about the service. That doesn't mean I wouldn't be flexible in cutting existing customers a favorable deal to sign a long-term contract.

– I think I almost believe you. Summarize for me.

My strategy would be three-pronged. One, keep IBM out by raising the barriers to entry. Two, do whatever it takes to keep our current customers. We talked about raising switching costs, increasing promotional efforts – things like customer loyalty programs and establishing long-term contracts. And finally, grow through acquisition and a major marketing effort.

– That was good.

- Type of Case: Competitive Response
- Comments: The three-pronged approach served the student well. He was able to lay out his strategy in a clear and logical manner that was simple and easy to follow. The student stood his ground when pushed about a price war. Whether you agree with him or not he articulated his point and stuck with it.

+ Starbucks

Case 5 : Wall Street wants to see Starbucks sales grow 30 percent annually for the next five years. The "street" has been telling Starbucks to open more coffee shops, but the coffee retailer feels it has exhausted all areas where it could grow. What should Starbucks do?

So Starbucks wants its sales to grow by 30 percent a year for the next five years.

– Yes.

Besides the growth in sales, are there any other objectives I should be aware of?

– No. I should add that I only want you to focus on the U.S. market.

Okay. How much did Starbucks grow last year, and what is the difference between growth of company sales and store sales?

– It had an increase of 26 percent from consolidated net revenues. Comparable store sales increased 10 percent.

So we're interested in growing Starbucks overall, not just increasing store sales?

– That's right.

Is the industry growing at around the same rate?

– Around the same.

What's Starbucks market share?

– Good question, but not relevant.

While I know that Wall Street would like to see us open more stores, that might not be the best solution to 30 percent growth. I'd like to break this problem down into two areas. Store growth and company growth. Because location is the key to success for any restaurant, if we are to open new stores we need to make sure that the location of the stores is great. But it sounds like Starbucks has been looking for great locations and is running out of sites. It's possible that the market might be close to saturation. If we're going to increase sales in this area we'd have to concentrate on taking away market share from our competitors and getting more revenues out of our existing stores.

So let's look at the existing stores. There are a couple of ways to increase sales. We could increase prices, run a marketing campaign to get more people into the stores, and try to get the customers who do come into the stores to spend more money.

You said that store sales only increased by 10 percent. I'll assume that some products far outsell others. That means that there are some dogs. We need to eliminate the products that sell poorly and replace them with new innovative products that will drive customers into the stores. We should also look at how individual stores are doing and close down the ones that

are losing money. For example, we might review the operating hours of each store and have certain stores stay open to serve late-night coffee drinkers, particularly stores in college towns and near movie theaters. We should also look to see if our competitors are doing anything new and ingenious.

– Okay. What else?

I'll assume that there is some elasticity in gourmet coffee prices. However, I'd like to check out the competitor's prices before I make a decision on that. But regardless, raising prices isn't enough to generate a 30 percent increase in company-wide sales.

– So what would you do?

If we are to increase sales for the company, we need to review some proven growth strategies. We can develop new products. Initiate a marketing campaign to tell the public about the new products. Increase our distribution channels. We can build sales through acquisition by acquiring a smaller competitor with great locations and products. Or we can expand outside the gourmet coffee industry.

I'd like to touch briefly on those.

– Sounds like a plan.

First, develop new products. This would include not only new drinks and food items, such as ice cream and prepared gourmet meals, but items like coffee makers and gift baskets.

– Starbucks already does that.

Oh. Well, what about reviewing the traffic flow of each store. So if they're slow during the lunch hours they can sell sandwiches. They could even get into catering. I'd have to review the current product line before I made a final report.

– Okay. What else?

Second, would be to develop a marketing campaign. Not only could we market the brand and new products, but possibly get involved in a social effort like Ben and Jerry's did. That action seemed to help their corporate image and sales figures.

– Possibly.

Third, increase distribution channels. We already talked about opening new stores if we can find the right locations. I'll assume that Starbucks has a Web site so they probably sell items over the Internet.

– That's right.

Other distribution channels might be through grocery stores, gourmet shops, large offices, university food services, and hotels. And as long as I'm brainstorming without commitment I'd like to throw out the idea of setting up an Avon or Tupperware-like home party.

– They already do all that except the home parties.

Fourth, we could build sales through acquisition of small regional competitors. Or we could buy up a chain of sandwich shops or restaurants and grow that way. Or we can establish and attach a dry cleaning service so that people can drop off their clothes and pick up a coffee. It would give them an additional reason to stop in.

– I have to tell you, you're not dazzling me yet. ⇒ stick to your guns...

It's because I haven't had my coffee yet. Have you?

– (laughs) Keep going.

Finally, Starbucks might want to look outside the industry to grow. Maybe focus money and investments in other high-growth industries.

– You want to summarize for me?

First, I think that 30 percent growth is possible. What Starbucks needs to do is stick with their current game plan of expansion. In addition, they need to review current products and stores, and get rid of the ones that aren't producing. They need to develop new products, and expand their distribution channels. One way to expand their channels is to look at making an acquisition within the industry.

Finally, they should investigate opportunities outside their current industry. See if there are any synergies to be had like shared customers, manufacturing or transportation.

– Interesting. Next time, drink your coffee before your interview.

- **Type of Case: Increase sales and growth.**

- **Comments: The student did well. While he didn't come up with anything really new, he did ask good questions. He also directed his answer away from just increasing the number of stores to alternative ways of growing the company.**

+ Snow Job

Case 6 : Snow Shovels Inc. (SSI) imports and distributes snow shovels. The snow shovel market is relatively stable. As expected, sales depend on demand and demand depends on weather. SSI has to order its shovels four months in advance. How many shovels should they order?

SSI imports and distributes snow shovels. They have to order their product four months in advance. They want to know how many shovels should they order?

– Yes.

Besides deciding how many shovels to order, are there any other objectives I should be concerned about?

– Yes. The goal is to maximize profits with the lowest amount of risk and the least amount of inventory on hand.

What areas of the country do they cover?

– Just Wellesley, Massachusetts.

I'd look at expanding into other areas.

– No. They just want to focus on their little corner of the world.

Then maybe we can increase their distribution channels. How many distribution channels do they have?

– Good question, but not relevant to what I'm looking for in this question.

How many did they order last year?

– Two thousand.

What was the weather like last year?

– Cold with lots of snow.

Did they have any inventory left over from the year before?

– Yes, five hundred shovels.

Is it fair to assume that they sold all 2500 shovels this past year?

– Yes.

So there is no left over inventory?

– That's right. SSI hates to carry over inventory.

Could we have sold more? Were there orders left unfilled?

– Yes. It's fair to say that if it's a cold winter they will sell 3,000 shovels. If it's a mild winter they will only sell 1,000.

Do we know what the forecast is for the coming winter?

– There is a 40 percent chance that it will be a cold winter and a 60 percent chance that the winter will be a mild.

Okay. Let me get this straight. There is a 40 percent chance of a cold winter in which we could sell 3,000 shovels. There's a 60 percent chance of a mild winter in which we would sell 1,000 shovels. And SSI hates to carry over inventory. How much do we pay for the shovels and how what do we charge?

– We buy them for $10 and sell them for $20.

So we make $10 a shovel. Let's figure that 40% of 3,000 equals 1,200 and 60% of 1,000 equals 600. If you add them together it equals 1,800 shovels.

– That's it? That's your answer? Why does everyone come up with 1800 shovels? I've given this case five times today and everyone has come up with 1800 shovels. Think about the information I gave you. Think about the objective.

I'd like to look at the estimated value. If we order a thousand shovels and assume that no matter what kind of winter we had we would still sell 1,000 shovels then the estimated value would be

# Ordered	# Sold	Income	Costs	Net	Times %	Expected Profit
1,000	1000	1000 X 20	1000 X 10	10,000	100%	$10,000
						$10,000

If we order 2,000 shovels and there is a 60 percent chance of a mild winter in which we will only sell 1,000 shovels and a 40 percent chance of a cold winter in which we would sell all 2,000 then it would be –

# Ordered	# Sold	Income	Costs	Net	Times %	Expected Profit
2,000	1000	1000 X 20	2000 X 10	0	60%	$0
2,000	2000	2000 X 20	2000 X 10	20,000	40%	$8,000
						$8,000

If we order 3,000 shovels and there is a 60 percent chance of a mild winter in which we will only sell 1,000 shovels and a 40 percent chance of a cold winter in which we would sell all 3,000 then it would be –

# Ordered	# Sold	Income	Costs	Net	Times %	Expected Profit
3,000	1000	1000 X 20	3000 X 10	(10,000)	60%	$(6,000)
3,000	3000	3000 X 20	3000 X 10	30,000	40%	$12,000
						$6,000

Based on the numbers above, and assuming that you're relatively risk adverse I would have to suggest that you order 1,000 shovels. You are pretty much guaranteed a $10,000 profit. If you order 3,000 shovels you have only a 40 percent chance of making $12,000 and a 60 percent chance of losing $6,000.

– Can you graph it?

Sure. It would look like this.

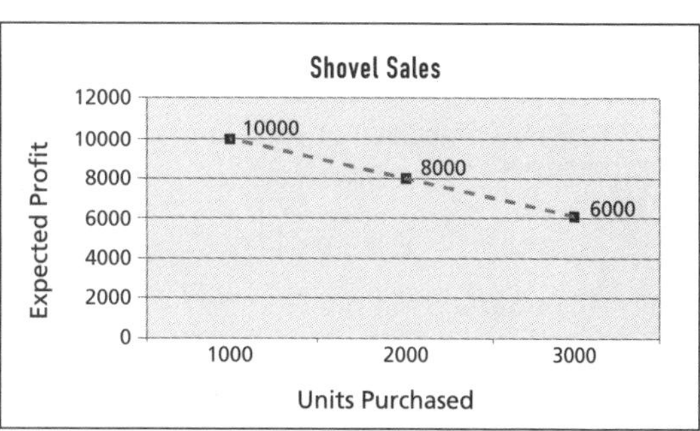

– Good recovery.

One last question. In this case we assumed that the leftover inventory is a loss in the current period? It's really an asset unless they plan to throw it away.

– Good point. You're right, but in this case we don't want to deal with it.

- **Type of Case: Strategy**

- **Comments: This case is all about risk. The student tried to come to a fast answer, then pulled back and quickly rethought this strategy based on the interviewer's reaction. Estimated value may not be common knowledge to a lot of non-MBAs so go back and reread the answer.**

Editor's note: I've given this case 25 times to Harvard students and only 2 got the correct answer. On a scale of 1 to 10 this is probably a 9.

expected value!

✛ Popcorn City

Case 7 : Our client recently purchased a popcorn manufacturing plant that packages popcorn for two mid-sized brands. Once he saw the margins, he decided to manufacture under his own brand. What does he need to do?

Just to make sure I understand, our client purchased a popcorn plant that currently packages popcorn for two mid-sized companies. After seeing how big the margins are he's decided to manufacture popcorn under his own brand. We need to advise him of a game plan. Are there any other objectives?

– Make profits.

How big are the margins?

– Ninety percent.

Is the industry growing?

– Yes. Americans spent $1.25 billion on 5 billion bags of microwave popcorn last year. That represents a six percent growth. They spent another $500 million on ready-to-eat popcorn. That puts popcorn fourth behind potato chips, tortilla chips and nuts as the most popular snack for men.

What about women?

– Women rate popcorn as their number one snack food.

There must be a lot of competition?

– Yes. The market leaders are Act II and Orville Redenbacher, which are both owned by ConAgra – a huge multinational. There are also a number of smaller players such as Popz, Jolly Time, Lil Chiefs, Pop Weaver and Pop Secret just to name a few.

One of our biggest challenges will be to differentiate ourselves from our competitors. How do we build brand? Would our products be much different from the competitors'?

– At his point I don't know. Maybe you can help us with that problem. That's why we hired your firm.

Okay, one major issue is building brand. I'd like to come back to that if possible.

– Sure.

Will we be producing just microwave popcorn?

– We would have several products. Currently he's manufacturing premium microwave popcorn in three flavors, premium traditional popcorn kernels in poly or plastic bags and traditional popcorn kernels in plastic jugs.

I think it's safe to say that our client knows the manufacturing side of the business. Some things we need to think about are how are we going to enter the market? I can't see that there would be any barriers to entry. It's not a regulated industry. The technology isn't proprietary. I'll assume that we'll have access to distribution channels. Do we have enough capital to introduce and market ourselves?

– Yes.

Let's take a minute to look at what our management team's like and figure out what their core competencies are? We're strong in manufacturing, but are probably weak in marketing and possibly sales. How is our sales department?

– Very, very small. We manufacture for two companies so there is not a lot of sales activity going on. The popcorn market is somewhat limited in that respect.

We need to think about who are our customers will be and how best can we reach them. And once they're our customers how do we gain their loyalty and retain them as clients? I'd also see if there is going to be a competitive response. Will one or both of the companies that we currently manufacturer for pull their business if we compete directly against them?

– Maybe. That's a good point.

If we are going to enter this market we need a full commitment. If our plant clients pull their business do we have enough cash on hand to ensure we can survive while we ramp up? If they do pull their business, it would probably take them several months to find a new manufacturer. What can we be doing now to keep them from leaving? How can we raise their switching costs? Or, does it make sense to buy one or both of them out?

– Do a cost benefit analysis for me.

If we start from scratch we'll have to one, find marketing and sales people. Two, establish distribution channels such as food brokers and distributors. Three, we need to find a few big customers fast – like a Wal-Mart or Costco. We could hire away our competitors' sales staff.

If we bought out a competitor they would have established distribution channels, management in place, and name recognition. It would save us a lot of time, but it would probably be expensive. Part of the decision would be based on our cash situation. It might be worth looking into.

If we didn't buy an established player we would have to build brand. We could increase our profile with a marketing and public relations campaign. One way to differentiate ourselves is through pricing. Selling at a lower price.

– Let's not talk pricing. We've already decided that we will be priced the same as our major competitors.

Then another way to differentiate our company is to donate a percentage of profits to a good cause. Ben and Jerry's Ice Cream donates approximately 8% of its pre-tax profits. As does

Stonyfield Farms Yogurt. Both those companies have received good press and increased sales from their association with good causes. Who do we see as our customers?

– Families. Women.

We could donate a portion of pre-taxed profits to a family-oriented literacy program. That's a special interest of First Lady Laura Bush. So it might draw additional attention and besides it's a great cause.

If I could, I might suggest that we cast our net wider and go after the kid and teen market as well. We could make some "rad" popcorn that pops in different colors – red, blue, green and yellow. Think of it as a microwave bag of M&M popcorn. Or, like Ben and Jerry's we could develop different flavored popcorn and give it funky names like they did with Cherry Garcia. We could offer single servings, the standard 3-serving packet as well as a party tub size.

– What else?

Let's talk about markets. I've been assuming that we are only talking about the US consumer market.

– Let's just keep this focused on the US market.

Okay, but there is also the institutional market like concession stands and the fundraising market. It's a way for schools and sports teams to raise money. These products along with gift baskets could be sold over the web site. Do we have a web site?

– Not yet.

I would put a lot of thought into the web site and make it fun as well as informative. We could also continue to package popcorn under other people's names. I know that Hollywood Video and Blockbuster have their own "brand' of popcorn. Let's go after those accounts. If there is a 90 percent margin then there is a lot room to move in regards to pricing.

– Any other marketing ideas?

Two. We could give General Electric packages to give away whenever someone buys a new microwave oven. We could also sell hotels and motels individual packages to have in their guest rooms with microwaves. There are a hundred and one ways to market this.

It seems like you're having fun with this question.

Yes. I love problems like this.

– Okay, summarize for me. What would you tell our client?

I'd tell them that this is a great market to be in, but in order to do well we have to overcome a few hurdles, particularly if they have decided to enter the market on their own and not buy their way in.

– Assume that we are, as you say, starting from scratch.

Then the biggest hurdle is differentiating ourselves from the competition. We need to come up with new products and expand beyond our targeted audience of families and women to include teens and preteens. Often, kids make the buying decisions regarding snack foods. We need to develop some "rad" types of popcorn flavors and names, i.e. Ben & Jerry's to get the kids interested. One way to attract women and families to our brand is to donate part of our pre-tax profits to a literacy foundation. Another way is to offer a variety of packaging sizes.

The next big hurdle is the marketing and sales side of the management team. I suggest we hire away some of our competitors' talent. They already have the contacts inside the big buyers like Wal-Mart and Costco. Not to mention inside information on what the competitor has done in the past and what they are planning to do in the future.

A third concern is protecting our current revenue stream. The two companies that we are currently producing popcorn for might get irked that we will now be competing directly against them. We need to make it hard for them to pull their business.

Finally, I would aggressively go after packaging opportunities of "house brands" like Blockbuster and Hollywood video. The margins won't be as great, but if we have plant capacity available, it's a good additional revenue stream.

– Excellent.

- Type: Starting a new business, entering a new market.
- Comments: This student hit a home run. She had a lot of good questions, a number of good ideas, and some insight into the market. She also got big points for thinking about ways to keep the current clientele from leaving our company once they find out that we will be competing directly against them.

+ Cow Brothers Premium Ice Cream

Case 8 : Cow Brothers is a maker of super premium ice cream, low-fat ice cream, low-fat yogurt, and sorbet. Its products are high quality and the company uses only natural ingredients. Cow Brothers products are distributed nationwide through supermarkets, grocery stores, convenience stores, franchises and company-owned ice cream shops, and restaurants.

Cow Brothers has 30 flavors and sells its products in one-pint containers. It also has single servings on a stick.

Cow Brothers has strong brand recognition. Its "Have a Cow" marketing campaign met with great success. Last year sales were $200 million ($177 million came from supermarket and grocery store sales), which put the company third in the industry behind Haagen Dazs and Ben & Jerry's. These top three competitors hold 62% of the market.

The president, Winston Cow, is still not satisfied. He wants to increase company sales to $250 million by next year. How do you do it?

Let me make sure I understand. Cow Brothers, the number three maker of premium ice cream, wants to increase its sales from $200 million to $250 million next year. That would be an increase of around 25%. How much did Cow Brothers' sales increase last year?

– 10%.

And that was mainly due to the "Have a Cow" marketing campaign?

– Yes.

One objective is to increase company sales. Are there any other objectives or goals that I should be aware of?

– No.

Is the company privately held? ? going public = more $ or what?

– Yes.

What was the overall industry growth last year?

– 12%.

So Haggen Daz and Ben & Jerry's only grew by 12% last year?

– No. Ben & Jerry's grew by 20%, Haagen Dazs by less.

First, we should analyze what Ben & Jerry's did to increase its sales, and compare it not only to what we did, but to what Haagen Dazs did as well.

– Fine. What else?

We need not only to increase sales, but also to grow the company. The three major ways to increase sales are to raise prices, get customers to buy more when they purchase Cow Brothers, and to expand our market base. Are we priced competitively?

– Our prices exactly match our competitors.

So that's a no for raising prices. You mentioned that Cow Brothers only produces ice cream in the one-pint containers. Have they thought about a two-pint container? That way customers would buy more per transaction.

– That's a possibility.

The third way is to expand our market base. I'd like to talk growth strategies. I know of five main growth strategies: increase distribution channels, increase product line, launch a major marketing campaign, diversify, and acquire a competitor. I'd like to look at the advantages and disadvantages of each of these and see which makes sense.

It seems as if we are tied into all the major distribution channels for our products. But there must be areas of the country where distribution is weak. I'd analyze those markets and see if we can't increase the number of outlets that carry our products.

Increase our product line: You said we have 30 flavors. How many flavors do the supermarkets and ice cream shops carry?

– The supermarkets carry five at a time, the ice cream shops carry 15.

We don't want to increase the number of flavors because no one can carry them as is. We need to add new sizes, not new flavors. You said that the "Have a Cow" marketing campaign went well. We should look at increasing our marketing budget.

The next idea is somewhat radical, but bear with me. Diversification. Cow Brothers has great brand recognition. It's well-known and stands for quality. In marketing class we read Ted Levitt's article "Marketing Myopia," in which he uses an example of the buggy whip company. When the car came along, the demand for buggy whips dropped significantly. If the buggy whip company saw itself as being in the transportation business instead of the buggy whip industry, it would still be in business today. Likewise, if Cow Brothers pictures itself in the dairy business or gourmet foods business, it can take better advantage of its brand name.

Cow Brothers might want to try a line of gourmet cheeses and cream cheeses. The cream cheeses could be distributed through all the regular distribution channels, but we could also create new distribution channels through various chains of bagels shops, which may also want to sell our single-serve ice cream products.

– That's food for thought.

Now, acquisition might be a possibility if we can get the idea funded without loading us up with debt. We might look to buy one of our lesser, regional competitors, particularly in an area of the country where our distribution channels and name recognition are weak.

– Okay, good. So what are your recommendations?

First, I'd continue and probably step up our marketing campaign. Second, I would increase our product line by offering a two-pint container size as well as the original one-pint size. I'd also diversify our product line into other dairy products, like gourmet cream cheeses, to take advantage of our brand name and our established distribution channels. Third, I'd analyze the possible acquisition of a regional competitor, particularly in a region of the country where our sales are weak. That way we can take advantage of their established distribution channels.

- **Type of case : Increasing sales and growing the company.**

- **Comments : First, she was quick to realize that this was a two-scenario case: increasing sales and growing the company. She also quickly figured out the client's expectations. Winston Cow wanted to increase company sales to $250 million. What kind of percentage did that represent? And was it feasible? Realizing that ice cream sales alone couldn't reach the client's goal, she looked at the company overall and assessed and changed its strategy. Finally, her ability to look outside the existing business led to a great idea—Cow Brothers Gourmet Cream Cheese.**

+ Jamaican Battery Enterprise

Case 9 : Our client is the Jamaican Battery Company. Currently, they sell car batteries throughout the Caribbean, Africa, and Central and South America. Over the past two decades they have been eyeing the Cuban battery market. However, Cuban Battery Enterprise, a state-owned battery company currently has 100 percent of the secondary market. The reason they have 100 percent of the secondary market is because the Cuban Government has a 50 percent tariff on the manufacturing costs and shipping costs all imported batteries.

The Castro government has just announced they will be lowering the tariff on batteries by 5 percent a year for the next 10 years until the tariff reaches zero.

The Jamaican Battery Board of Directors wants to know the size of the Cuban market and if, when and how they should enter it.

The Board of Directors of the Jamaican Battery Company wants to know the size of the Cuban market and if, when and how they should enter it. We know that currently the Cuban battery market is dominated by the Cuban Battery Enterprise because of a 50 percent tariff on the manufacturing and shipping costs on all imported batteries. But we also know that the Government is lowering the tariff by 5 percent a year for the next 10 years until the tariff reaches zero.

– Yes, that's right.

I'll assume that the objective is to gain market share and be profitable. Are there any other objectives that I should know about?

– No.

What is the market share that they would like?

– One hundred percent.

Let me rephrase, what is the market share that they can reasonably expect to gain and under what time table?

– Twenty five percent within 5 years of entering.

Let's start by estimating the size of the Cuban secondary car battery market. I'll assume that there are 10 million people in Cuba.

– That's a little low, but a good figure to use.

I'll also assume that disposable income is limited and that only one in ten households has a car. So if we estimate that the average Cuban household is made up of five people –

– Where did you get five from?

I'm assuming that there are two generations living in a number of the homes.

– Okay.

So if there are 2 million households and if only one in ten have a car that means that there are 200,000 cars. I would also like to add in another 10,000 vehicles which include taxis, trucks, and government vehicles.

– So 210,000 vehicles.

Yes. I'll also assume that Cubans keep their cars for a long time and that the average car needs a new battery every three years.

– Three years? What were you thinking when you made that assumption?

I was assuming that this is a monopoly in a Communist country, thus the quality of the battery might not be competitive with a Jamaican Battery which probably lasts five years.

– Go on.

So 210,000 vehicles will need a new battery every three years. But there are two factors we need to figure in. First, let's say that half of the 10,000 "other" vehicles that we mentioned are government or military vehicles. So we need to subtract 5,000 from the total. Now it is 205,000 divided by every three years equals around 68,000 batteries.

Also the number is going to be reduced over the long run because our batteries will last five years, not three. I'm not sure how to factor that in.

– That's okay. It's just important that you brought it up.

If we want 25 percent of that market we're talking 17,000 batteries a year.

– Okay, what's next?

I'd like to know some costs and prices. What are our costs and prices compared to theirs?

– Prices are irrelevant, but costs aren't. It costs the Cuban Battery Enterprise $12 to produce a battery. Their raw material costs are 20 percent, their labor costs are 50 percent and their overhead and all other costs are 30 percent.

It costs us $9 to produce a battery. Our raw material costs are 20 percent, our labor costs our 25 percent and all other costs including overhead and marketing is 55 percent. It costs us $1 to ship it to Cuba.

Let me just write this out.

Cuban Battery Enterprise		**Jamaican Battery Company**	
Production costs:	$12	Production costs:	$9
Raw material	20%	Raw material	20%
Labor	50%	Labor	25%
All other costs	30%	All other costs	30%
Shipping costs	$0	Shipping costs	$1
Tariff	$0	Tariff	$5
Total cost	$12	Total cost	$15

That means it cost us $9 manufacturing cost plus $1 shipping costs which equals $10. Add in the 50 percent tariff and we're talking $15 a battery.

We now need to figure out when we will be competitive. In five years the tariff will drop from 50 percent to 25 percent which is half. So it will still cost us $10 to manufacturer and ship the battery, however, the tariff will only be $2.50. That makes our total cost $12.50. So I would say based on sheer numbers we can enter and compete during year six. But if we can market and explain that for a little bit more our battery will last five years instead of three years we might be able to charge a premium and that could justify entering the market in year five.

– Let's switch hats for a second. You now are advising the Cuban Battery Enterprise. What do you advise them?

My first step is to approach the government and try to get them to reconsider lowering the tariff.

– Castro's mind is made up. The tariff will be reduced.

Next, I would want to find out why our labor costs are so high.

– Why do you think?

The two things that jump to mind are technology and medical costs. Maybe our technology is old and our manufacturing process is very labor intensive.

– Yes, that's part of it. What else?

We are in a communist country where healthcare is free. That's the hidden cost in everything that's done, every service, and every manufactured item. Even countries like Canada with its national healthcare program have higher prices. If the Canadian dollar wasn't so weak compared to the US dollar they would price themselves right out of the market in many items.

– We'll save that discussion for another time.

Well, we can't do much about the healthcare costs, but we can upgrade our technology. The upgrade would also make our batteries more competitive and able to last five years instead of three years.

– Say we upgrade our technology and we are now able to make a world class battery for $9 a battery. How would that change things?

Well the tariff becomes moot in the sense that we can be competitive without it. Which is good, but we still have a perception problem. I think we need to launch a marketing campaign to show the Cuban public that we have a new battery that is world class. I'd also like to review our customer service and our distribution channels. These are key functions that are often overlooked in a monopoly environment.

– Good point. Our customer service is pitiful and our distribution channels are restricted to two major warehouses, one in Havana and the other in Nuevitas. You said that you would launch a marketing campaign and I'll assume that there will be a customer service aspect to that. What would you do about the distribution channels?

I'll make two assumptions. First, I'll assume that we have at least two years before the Jamaican Battery Company enters our market. Second, I'll assume that other non-American battery companies will also enter our market, probably about the same time and with a similar strategy to the Jamaican company.

– Both fair assumptions.

First I would go to every gas station on the island, both in the cities and in the countryside. I would front them the cost of the batteries, give them a nice display rack, free t-shirts, and maybe some cash. In return they would have to sign an exclusive agreement to sell only our batteries.

Let me ask you this? Does the government make their own tires? And if yes, how's the quality?

– Yes they do, but the quality is poor. However based on your advice they will also upgrade their technology and launch a marketing plan because the tire tariff is being eliminated as well.

So you know what I'm getting at. We can open a service store where residents can get both a new battery and new tires, and maybe an oil change. We can snap up all the best locations before the foreign competitors come into our market.

– We're switching hats again. You are now back to advising the Jamaican Battery Company. You have seen that the Cuban Battery Enterprise has upgraded its plant, increased its distribution channels, formed a joint venture with the Cuban Tire Enterprise and has launched a nationalistic marketing campaign. Do you now enter the Cuban battery market, if so how?

Whenever you enter a new market there are several things you need to examine. Who are the major players? What size market share do they have? How are their products or services different from ours? And are there any barriers to entry? The major player is the Cuban Battery Enterprise. They have 100 percent of the market. Two years ago their products were inferior, but today they are very similar. The tariff was a barrier to entry, but now it looks as if access to distribution channels could be a threat.

I've learned that there are three main ways to enter a market. Start from scratch, buy your way in, or form a joint venture. I'd like to do a quick cost benefit analysis of each. Start from scratch would be a fine strategy if we can define our distribution channels. If the Cuban firm has all the gas stations tied up and have built tire and battery stores then our distribution means are limited. Plus, selling 17,000 batteries a year might not justify an investment of building our own battery stores.

The second strategy is to buy our way in. Since this is a communist country there isn't a lot of buying opportunity. If we were going to buy anyone it would have been the Cuban Enterprise, and we should have bought it when they were a mess and not a formidable competitor.

The third way is to form a joint venture. If I work under the assumption that there are no independent battery distributors, then my first choice is to form a joint venture with one of the tire companies that are entering the market. My guess is that there will be several tire companies and battery companies jumping in, so we need to be part of that coalition.

– So it all boils down to –

So it all boils down to distribution channels.

– Great job.

- **Type of Case: Strategy / entering a new market / market sizing**

- **Comments: This was a long case and one that you'd get in the final rounds where you have about an hour to answer it. It had a market sizing component to it, but probably the hardest thing was the switching of the hats. It forced the student to come up with counterstrategies to the strategies he just developed.**

Most students would have tried to figure out the reduction in tariff fees year by year, but this student saved time and impressed the interviewer by picking a point in the middle and working from there. He made the math simple and was able to do the calculations in his head.

The student was very well organized, he even wrote out the costs and percentages in a little chart. This impresses the interviewer and makes everything easy for the student to find when flipping back through his notes.

+ Coke

Case 10 : Coca-Cola is trying to boost profitability domestically by raising its prices. It's focusing on the grocery store market where the volume is high, but the margin is low. What are the economics of raising the prices and is this a good idea?

So Coke plans to increase profitability by raising prices. They want to know if that's a good idea.

– That's right.

I know that raising profitability is their main objective. Are there other objectives that I should be aware of?

– They don't want to lose market share.

Are we just focusing on Coke and not any of their other brands?

– You can think of all Coke products as one product, Coke.

What's Coke's current market share?

– Not relevant to the question.

How much does it cost to make a can of Coke?

– Not relevant to the question.

How many cans does Coke sell to U.S. grocery stores and at what price?

– Coke sold 100,000,000 cans at 23 cents each to grocery stores last year. If prices remain stable, they expect volume growth of 6 percent. They want to raise the price to 27 cents per can and they forecast volume growth of only 1 percent.

Let's see. First I can multiply:

100 million cans times .27 times 1.01 = 27,270,000
100 million cans times .23 times 1.06 = 24,380,000
2,890,000

So even though they would be selling 5 million less cans of Coke, they'd be making more of a profit, about three million dollars more.

– Profitability would be boosted by what percent?

I can take 27 minus 24 equals 3 divided by 24 equals approximately 12 percent.
So by raising prices and selling less, Coke can boost its sales by approximately 12%.

– To maintain market share Coke needs to stir up consumer demand with a major marketing campaign to raise brand awareness and focus on lifestyle issues. Knowing that, and if you were Pepsi, what would you do?

Pepsi has three choices. It can follow Coke's lead and raise its prices to match Coke's. It can leave prices the way they are, or it can take advantage of the price change and lower its price.

If Coke spends a fortune marketing its product and it does its job and gets people into the stores, Pepsi can snatch sales away at the last minute with a lower price. We are talking grocery stores here. Women do most of the buying in grocery stores and are often price conscious. If they saw two brand name colas, Pepsi and Coke and if Coke sold for $2.99 a 12-pack compared to $2.59 for a 12-pack of Pepsi then most shoppers would choose the one on sale or the one with the lower price.

Pepsi might even want to lower its price so it can increase its market share.

In sailing, if you are behind, you're not going to catch up with or beat the opponent by sailing the same course. You have to take a different tact. So if Pepsi lowers its prices and cuts marketing costs it can steal customers away from Coke through in-store promotions and point of contact displays.

– So if you were Pepsi, what would you do?

Let's run some numbers. How many cans does Pepsi sell to grocery stores.

– Pepsi sells 80 million cans at 23 cents a piece.
If Pepsi follows Coke and raises its prices its volume will drop from 6 to 3 percent.
If Pepsi keeps its price the same, its volume will increase from 6 to 12 percent.
If Pepsi lowers its prices to 21 cents, Pepsi's volume will increase from 6 to 20 percent.

80,000,000 X 1.03 = 82,400,000 X .27 = 22,248,000
80,000,000 X 1.12 = 89,600,000 X .23 = 20,608,000
80,000,000 X 1.20 = 96,000,000 X .21 = 20,160,000

I'd follow Coke's lead.

– Even if you knew that Coke's volume would rise from 1 percent to 3 percent.

Yes.

– Interesting. Thanks.

- **Type of case: Strategy based on numbers.**
- **Comments: Straightforward case once you have the numbers.**

you better know how to do this!

✢ World Spacelines

Case 11 : World Spacelines has developed a rocket-boosted spaceplane" that can take off and land like a conventional airplane, but can also fly through the atmosphere and orbit the earth. World Spacelines wants to take passengers on a three-hour tour of space. They have built a prototype, which cost them $500 million. Each additional spaceplane will cost $100 million to manufacture.

- **Estimate the size of the domestic market.**
- **Determine what price they should charge for a ticket.**
- **How many spaceplanes should they build in the future?**
- **Should they manufacture spaceplanes for the competition?**

So let me make sure I understand. World Spacelines has developed a spaceplane that can take-off and land like a conventional plane and it's designed to take tourists on a three-hour tour of space.

– Yes.

You'd like me to estimate the size of the U.S. market, determine what to charge customers, decide how many of these spaceplanes to build, and whether or not they should manufacture them for our competitors.

– That's right.

I'll assume one objective is to build a successful business. Any other objectives I should be aware of?

– Yes. They want to be the first organization to build a space hotel.

Are there any competitors?

– No.

Do we have a patent on our technology?

– Yes.

How long before someone weasels around the patent and starts to compete with us?

– Three years.

How big is the plane? How many passengers does it hold?

– One hundred.

The trip takes three hours. How many trips per day are you planning?

– Two trips a day, 360 days a year.

Well before I can estimate the market size I need to know the price we are going to charge. Because if it's one dollar then the market is just about the whole country. But if we charge one million dollars then the market is much, much smaller.

And before I can figure out the price I need to know what it's going to cost us per passenger. So I'm going to make some assumptions about costs. How long is the life of the plane?

– Twenty years. And yes, you can allocate the costs over twenty years without interest. What do you think the major costs are?

I figure the major costs are the cost of the plane, labor (both on-board and administrative), maintenance, fuel, airport fees, insurance and marketing.

– Good. I'll give you most of the costs, however I want you to figure out the fuel costs. The plane burns 10 gallons of fuel for every mile and the fuel costs $10 a gallon.

How far is our trip? How high is the sky?

– The Earth's atmosphere is about 300 miles thick, but most of the atmosphere (about 80%) is within 10 miles of the surface of the Earth. There is no exact place where the atmosphere ends; it just gets thinner and thinner, until it merges with outer space. In addition, we use very little fuel when we are orbiting and descending. So we'll estimate our trip goes 500 miles.

So 10 gallons per mile times 500 miles equals 5,000 gallons, times $10 a gallon is $50,000 per trip. You said two trips per day, 360 days a year. Okay, $100,000 per day times 360 days equals $36 million a year in fuel costs.

Major annual costs are: Prototype	
Cost of the plane	25,000,000
Labor (on-board & admin)	2,000,000
Maintenance	4,000,000
Fuel	36,000,000
Gate & Airport	1,000,000
Insurance	2,000,000
Marketing	2,000,000
TOTAL COSTS	72,000,000

Our costs are $72 million. We need to divide that by the number of passengers. You said 720 flights per year and 100 passengers per flight, which equals 72,000 passengers a year. Divide 72,000 passengers into $72 million in costs and you get $1,000 per passenger.

– Good. So what are you going to charge per trip?

Well there are three main pricing strategies. Competitive analysis, cost-based pricing, price-based costing. There is no competition so we have nothing to compare it to, except maybe exotic vacations, but that's a far reach. As far as cost-based pricing goes, our costs are $1,000, so if we double that to $2,000 that's a pretty good margin. However, this is really a special

trip. To go where no tourist has gone before, to a place that has been accessible to only a few elite astronauts. To a place that everyone has wondered about, not to mention all the trekkies. I think price-based costing is the way to go.

– So, what are you going to charge?

I'd like to figure out what the market is for $10,000 a ticket. Let's start with 250 million Americans. I'll assume that 2 percent of the population make over a hundred thousand a year and can afford a $10,000 vacation. So 2 percent of 250 million is 5 million people. Out of that 5 million maybe 20 percent would want to do it. So that's a base of a million customers.

How long does it take to build another spaceplane?

– Each spaceplane takes six months to build.

We have one plane now that we estimate that we can fill for the next 14 years. So I would build as many planes as I could at least for the next three years. Until we see what the competition is like, then reevaluate at that point.

– Really? I think your assumptions are a little too broad. Lay it out for me.

YEARS 1-5

PLANES	Y1	Y2	Y3	Y4	Y5
Plane 1	72K	72K	72K	72K	72K
Plane 2	36K	72K	72K	72K	72K
Plane 3	0	72K	72K	72K	72K
Plane 4	0	36K	72K	72K	72K
Plane 5	0	0	72K	72K	72K
Plane 6	0	0	36KK	72K	72K
Passengers	108K	252K	396K	432K	432
Total	108K	108K	360K	756K	1188
Running Total		360K	756K	1188K	1620

By the end of Year 3 we will have 6 planes up and running and we would have carried a total of 756,000 passengers, well below the 1 million market estimate. However, by the end of year four, even without any addition planes our running total climbs to almost 1.2 million passengers. That's 1.6 million passengers the following year. Two things can happen. First, we can lower the ticket price to $5,000 a ticket which would spike demand. Second, our other objective is to build a space hotel, so we will need space planes to shuttle people back and forth, provided the space hotel has been built by then. Even if it hasn't been built, the new demand will continue to fill our planes. Third, even though we haven't spoken about this, I think that there will be large international demand as well.

You also said that competition might show up around this time.

– That's right. The last question I asked was whether you'd sell spaceplanes to the competition?

Our revenues off the prototype would be $10,000 times 72,000 customers which equals $720,000,000 minus our costs of 72 million which equals $648 million for the first year. If each additional plane costs $100 million that's going to drop our costs by at least $20 million if not more, depending on shared costs. But let's reduce our costs by $20 million. So now we have revenues of $720 million minus costs of $52 million equals $668 million. For us to sell our spaceplanes to the competition wouldn't be practical. If we're making $668 million a year off of each plane we'd have to sell them for like 2 billion dollars. I doubt that the competition would pay that kind of money.

To answer your questions, the market size is 1 million passengers at $10,000 a ticket. If we drop it to $5,000 we'll see a huge spike in potential customers. I'd build as many planes as I could for the next three years then reevaluate our situation once we see what the competition is doing and how far along the construction is on our space hotel. And I wouldn't manufacture space planes for anyone but us.

- **Type of Case: Market-sizing, entering a new market, and pricing.**
- **Comments: Big points for realizing that she couldn't estimate the market size without first knowing the price of the ticket, and she couldn't estimate the price without first knowing the costs.**

Savannah Jane's Laundromat

Case 12 : You just bought Savannah Jane's Laundromat in Savannah, Georgia. It's twenty years old and had a small loss last year. What are you going to do?

Why did I buy it?

– Your consulting interviews didn't work out so you thought you'd take a shot at turning this business around, make some money and prove to the interviewers that they were wrong about you.

Has it been profitable in the past?

– Yes, but it has been on the decline over the last five years.

Why is that?

– Why do you think?

I'll assume that the former owner let things go. That maybe the washers and dryers are old and break down a lot. The place is probably dingy and not an attractive place to visit.

– That's pretty much it.

What kind of area am I in?

– You're in a strip mall. There's a liquor store, a discount clothing store, a sports bar, a real estate office and a bank.

Is the rest of the strip mall run down as well?

– No. I should also mention that you are not far from the Savannah College of Art and Design.

I am going to make the assumption that I did my due diligence and that the population and demographics are such that there is enough traffic to support a business.

– Yes, that's a fair assumption.

The first thing I'm going to do is inspect the equipment and determine the age and condition of each machine. I'll visit the bank and get a loan to fix up the place. I'll replace the equipment that needs it. I'll clean the place from top to bottom, repaint, and put in a new carpet. I'll stick in comfortable chairs, a wall television; get cable and a DVD player. We need to make it so that people will want to come and stay.

– Why stay?

You lose time and customers if people have to wait for a machine to free up. People who leave and come back often make others wait for their machine.

– Not me. When I was in college and grad school I never waited. If they weren't back in time I'd just throw their clothes on the floor.

Maybe you should have been an investment banker.

– (Laughs) I wasn't mean enough. Go on.

I would put in additional revenue generators such as vending machines, not only for soap and laundry stuff, but snacks and drinks. I'd offer a fluff and fold option where people could just drop off their clothes and then pick them up at the end of the day – pay by the pound.

– So you'd have employees?

Part-time employees, so I wouldn't have to pay them benefits.

– Maybe you should be the investment banker.

(Laughs) Ouch. I need to think about who my customers are. For the most part I think that they are mothers with young children, students, and non-student singles.

– That's fair.

During the day we probably get mothers and their children. For the children I'd put in books and Lego® sets. Maybe have a smaller TV with a VCR and some kid tapes. I'd encourage groups of mothers to meet there on certain days, maybe have a group that comes and watches certain soap operas every Tuesday and Friday. I'd put in a coffee bar, sell magazines and have internet access, that sort of thing.

I would let the students from the Savannah College of Art and Design display their art work and try to sell it. I'd do a trade out with some of the musicians at the college so that they could play their guitar or piano during certain hours and get to wash their clothes for free. Which reminds me; I'd offer a loyalty program and scan cards so that people wouldn't have to carry change all the time.

I'd work with the sports bar. Patrons could drop their laundry off and watch a sporting event and then pick it up on their way home.

– So you'd be open late?

With this customer base you'd have to be. I'd investigate on becoming a drop off point for a local dry cleaner as an additional revenue stream. Once I have everything in place I'd begin my marketing campaign and have a grand opening. I'd invite the press, maybe put up one of those signs – under new management.

– Okay good. Why don't you summarize for me.

I'd remodel, add revenue streams, watch costs, market creatively, and focus on customer service.

– Would you consider doing something like this if you don't get a consulting job?

Yes, I would. I think it would be fun, I'd learn a lot and make some good money along the way - but I still want to be a consultant.

- **Type of Case: Strategy / marketing / turnaround / acquisition**
- **Comments: The student did a good job. He showed that he could roll with the punches and maintain a sense of humor. He had some creative ideas and a plan. His summary might have been a little short for some folks, but he hit on all the major points without dwelling on them and being redundant.**

+ Hair-raising

Case 13 : Our client is a large pharmaceutical company that has developed a cure for baldness. It's a pill that will rapidly (within three months) regrow your hair to the thickness that it was when you were 15. The pill, which is called IPP2, needs to be taken every day to maintain that thickness. Please estimate the market size of the U.S. market and tell me how you would price the drug.

So our client is a large drug company that has developed a pill that will regrow hair. The product is called IPP2, and it needs to be taken daily. You want me to estimate the size of the market and also develop a pricing strategy.

– Yes, that's right.

One objective is to make a profit. Are there any other objectives I should keep in mind?

– No.

Okay, let's tackle the market size first. I'm going to assume that there are 240 million people in the U.S.; and I'm going to assume that the life expectancy of an American is 80 years. And I'm going to assume that there are even numbers of people in each age category. I'll break them down by generation. So 240 divided by four equals 60 million people in each age category. I'll assume that the breakdown between men and women is 50/50. I'll also assume that as men get older, a greater percentage of them grow bald.

	Men		Women	
1 –20 year olds	30m	0%	30m	0%
21–40 year olds	30m	25%	30m	1%
41–60 year olds	30m	50%	30m	2%
61–80 year olds	30m	75%	30m	3%

Before I go any further. Are there any side effects that would prevent any man or woman from taking the drug?

– Yes. It causes sexual dysfunction in 2% of men, and women thinking of having children shouldn't take it because it can cause birth defects.

I don't think that that is enough to deter men. However, we need to eliminate all women 40 years old and under. So, let's figure this out.

Men : 7.5 million + 15 million + 22.5 million = 45 million men
Women : 600 thousand + 900 thousand = 1.5 million women

So let's round up and say that our market is 50 million Americans.

– Fine.

Now, how would we price it? I'd like to look at it three different ways. First, who is our competition and what do they charge? Second, we'll look at cost-based pricing. And third, price-based costing.

Who is our competition, and what do they cost?

– There are two major competitors. One is a topical solution that sells for $60 for a month's supply. The second is a pill that sells for $50 for a month's supply.

How do we compare to our competitors in overall effectiveness?

– We are three times more effective.

Were there heavy R&D costs?

– No. This is actually the same drug that we produce for another illness. So research was minimal.

What is the cost of producing the drug and packaging it?

– The cost of the entire package is $1 for a month's supply.

One dollar? That's great. So with production costs of one dollar and no heavy R&D costs, then we can dismiss cost-based pricing. If we look at price-based costing, we need to figure out what the market will bear. How much will people be willing to pay for a full head of hair? Currently, they are paying $50 to $60 a month, but our product is three times better. So does that mean that they'll be willing to pay $150 a month or $5 a day? For the price of a sandwich, you could have a full head of hair. You're growing a little thin on top, sir. What would you pay?

– Rule number one, never insult the interviewer.

Sorry. But on you it looks good.

– And you were doing so well. What else do you have–regarding pricing?

We could go in below our competitors, then knock them out of the market, then crank the price once we've hooked them. Kind of like the gasoline pricing strategies of Standard Oil during the 1930s. But I don't think we'll need to do that. If the product is that effective, we'll get heavy press and soon drive the competition out of the market.

I would price it at $100 a month. That's $3.33 a day, the price of a Starbuck's coffee. That's just a little less than a 10,000% mark-up. So let's say that 50% of the bald men and women buy our product. That means revenues of $1,200 x 25 million equals a $30-billion-dollar-a-year product with very little marketing costs.

The last thing I'd like to point out is that we are not cannibalizing our future sales, because the user has to take the pill every day to maintain the full head of hair.

- **Type of Case : Market sizing, pricing.**
- **Comments : Our candidate was lucky that the interviewer had a sense of humor. He did a good job breaking down the market-sizing aspect of the case. He also looked at three pricing strategies, quickly dismissing one as irrelevant. Overall, a nice job.**

+ Pay Phones

Case 14 : Our client is a major player in the pay phone industry. Despite a 20% increase in market share, the manufacturer has experienced a decline in profits. The CEO wants to know why and what can be done about it.

Let me make sure I understand. Our client manufactures pay phones. Its market share has risen 20%, yet its profits are declining. The CEO wants to know why and what can be done about it.

– That's right.

Besides identifying and correcting the problem are there any other objectives I should be aware of?

– No. If you can do those two things I'll be happy.

What sort of market share does the company have and how has that increased?

– Currently it has 55%, up from 35% two years ago.

So they've increased their market share 20% in two years?

– That's right.

That's incredible. Wait. I'll assume that the overall market size of pay phones has dropped because of the increase in cell phones. Is that a fair assumption?

– Yes. Pay phone orders have dropped by 15% during that same two-year time period.

Have any pay phone manufacturers dropped out of the race?

– Yes, two.

And is that the main reason why we've gained so much market share?

– Yes. One of the reasons.

What are some others?

– You tell me.

Increased marketing, maybe special contracts, such as military contracts. We've probably lowered our price which has been cutting into our profit margin.

– Good. What's next?

How are our costs?

– Don't make me answer this case for you.

I'll assume that costs have increased. Particularly labor, marketing, parts, and especially transportation costs with the rise in fuel costs.

– That's right.

I'll also assume that the manufacturing process is pretty automated.

– That's right. You're not going to squeeze out much cost savings there.

Well I believe that the pay phone market is going to get worse before it gets better, if it ever does get better. But the public will always need pay phones. Maybe we need to change what they need the phone for. Currently, people use pay phones when their cell phone batteries are too low, when they don't have a cell phone or when their cell phone coverage doesn't reach a particular area of the country, or when they don't want the call to be traced back to them...

– Hopefully you've been watching too many cop shows.

Yeah. (laughs) Let's say I'm in New Orleans for the first time and my New England cell phone plan doesn't cover the Big Easy. Yet, I'm looking for a place to eat, sip a Hurricane and listen to some Dixieland Jazz. What if I could go to a pay phone and this pay phone has an LED display and touch screen. Now I'm looking for a restaurant so I drop a quarter and hit a button that says restaurants. Now the pay phone comes up with a list of restaurants and rates them. For that same quarter it connects me with the restaurant and asks if I want directions. I hit yes and a set of directions prints out. All this for my one quarter. Now restaurants or any company can place an ad which pops up as I hit restaurants as well as ads printed on the back of the directions tape like grocery stores do with their receipt tape.

– So you're saying turn a pay phone into an Internet connection.

Yes. It seems like the technology is already there, it's just a problem of conversion and phone design.

– We have about two minutes left.

Okay, let me review. The industry is shrinking and costs are rising. That, along with the fact that we've lowered our prices has led us to greater market share, but lower profit margins. Now we can bail from the market and try to diversify into another technology, or we can try to change the industry standard and bring it up to speed with the future of telecommunications.

– So what would you recommend?

I'd focus on costs, you can always reduce costs somewhere. I'd look to diversify into a growth industry to lessen the company's overall risk, and then I'd reinvent the pay phone as we described. And oh, the other thing I'd do is to ship the old inventory, the current pay phones, to developing countries.

– Thanks.

- **Type of case:** Increasing the bottom line, growing the company.

- **Comments:** The candidate was quick to figure out why the company's market share was increasing, yet the profits were falling. He also proved that he was quick to think on his feet – thinking outside the box. And the interviewer also gave him points for introducing a three-prong strategy, reduce costs, new product development and company diversification.

+ Brazilian Soda Manufacturer

Case 15 : You are working for a Brazilian soda manufacturer that has experienced declining profits over the last two years. Why do you think this is occurring? What are the company's options for improving profitability? What are the possible effects of a change in the soda's price? And oh yes, estimate for me the size of the soda market in Brazil.

Our client is a soda manufacturer in Brazil. For the last two years they have been experiencing a decline in profits. We want to know why, and what can be done about it. We also need to investigate the effects of a price change and finally you would like me to estimate the size of the Brazilian soda market. Besides increasing profits, are there any other objectives I should be concerned with?

– No, I think you have enough on your plate.

I have a few questions. Who are the major players in the Brazilian soda market? How much market share does each player have? And what are the current price differences in our products?

– Of course Coke and Pepsi are there. Together they make up 80 percent of the market. We have 10 percent and two generic brands that make up the remainder. Currently the retail pricing is as follows: A 12 ounce Coke and Pepsi sells for 80 cents US, our 12 ounce can sells for 50 cents, and the generics sell for 35 cents.

Do we sell for less because our name isn't as big or the quality of our product isn't as good?

– We like to think name recognition.

What's our product mix? How many flavors of soda do we sell?

Two, a cola and guarana – it's like a fruit soda.

And our competition?

Coke and Pepsi have a full array of products. The rest just make cola.

How is the soda market doing overall?

– It was up 10 percent.

Did we lose market share? Or is it just our profits that are declining?

– Good question. Our market share has remained the same.

Okay. Right now I'd like to take a stab at the size of the market. I'm not sure what the population of Brazil is.

– Take a guess.

Two hundred million.

– Very close. It's around 180 million, but why don't you use 200.

I'll assume that the population of Brazil is 200 million. I'm going to break it down by groups. But first I'll also assume that there are even numbers of people in each age group, so there is the same number of 10-year olds as there are 40 years olds. And I'll assume that the life expectancy is 80 years.

– The life expectancy is a little high, but go ahead.

Well I'm going to assume 50 weeks in a year.

– That explains it. Okay.

I want to break it down this way.

Age Group	Number of people	Soda drinkers	Sodas /week	Sodas / year
0–10	25 m	5 m	10	2.5 b
11–20	25 m	20 m	10	10 b
21–40	50 m	40 m	10	20 b
41–60	50 m	25 m	3	3.75 b
60 –80	50 m	10 m	2	1 b
Totals	200m	100m		37.25 b

Therefore, we can assume that the market is about 40 billion sodas a year. We have 10 percent or 4 billion cans of soda a year. How much do we make on each soda?

– It averages out to 25 cents US.

So we make $1 billion.

– Yes.

Four billion cans of soda a year, have we been able to meet demand? Are there any capacity constraints?

– No. We can handle it. However, if it goes much higher we'll have to add a second shift.

There can be several reasons why we are experiencing declining profits. It could be a drop in revenues, it could be our sales are flat, or our expenses are rising. I'd like to go through each of these.

– I can save you some time. We've looked at our manufacturing costs and have determined that they are not out of line. There have been increases, but they're small. In addition, we have done everything we could to reduce them.

You said our market share is the same, and that the industry is growing, so I'll assume that our sales aren't flat.

– That's a good assumption.

Well, if our manufacturing costs are in line and our sales are growing, then it might be a drop in revenues. You said we are making 25 cents per can of soda. Were we making more than that it in prior years?

– Yes. Good. Each of the last two years the distributor has raised his fee a penny a can a year. This year alone it cost us an additional $10 million on top of the $9 plus million from last year. We chose not to past the cost on to the retailer or the consumer.

Well maybe it's time. Your original question asked about the effects of pricing. There seems to be a big gap between the majors like Coke and Pepsi, which sell their product for 80 cents, our products which sell for 50 cents and the generics which sell theirs for 35 cents. Do we know what affect on volume an increase or decrease in prices will play?

– Use the original pricing of 25 cents a can. If we increase our prices by 5 cents, and assume that these changes will filter down to the consumer, we can expect a 5 percent loss in volume. If we leave our prices alone we can expect a 5 percent increase in volume. And if we lower our prices by 5 cents we can expect a 10 percent increase in volume.

If the percentage decrease in the quantity demanded is less than the percentage increase in the price, we have a net increase in revenues so the price increase makes sense. Similarly if the percentage increase in demand is greater than the percentage decrease in the price, we again have a net increase in revenues and so the price decrease makes sense.

– Why don't you show me?

You said we sell 4 billion cans of soda a year, so:

Present volume	D in volume	New volume	New price	Revenues
4 billion	- 5 percent	3.8 billion	.30	1.14 billion
4 billion	+ 5 percent	4.2 billion	.25	1.05 billion
4 billion	+10 percent	4.4 billion	.20	880 million

It looks as though choice one is the best. We'd be producing 400 million less cans, but making $90 million more than if we kept our prices the same and had a 5 percent boost in volume. In addition, we won't have to add that second shift. The worst thing we can do is to lower our prices.

Do we have any addition revenue streams? Do we produce anything besides soda?

– No. Don't go there. Just focus on soda manufacturing.

Then I'd summarize by saying that we determined the size of the Brazilian soda market to be 40 billion cans of soda a year, of which we produce 10 percent or 4 billion cans. We've determined that our profits are declining mainly because the distributors have increased their distribution fees by two pennies over the course of two years. This increase has cost us almost 20 million dollars. Now we can look for new distributors, but my assumption is that we don't have a lot of choice. So we increase our prices by 5 cents, this means we will produce 400 million less cans of soda and make 90 million dollars more. In addition, we will save on production costs, i.e. labor and raw materials, shipping costs, and the distributor fees.

– Very good.

- **Type of Case:** Market-sizing, pricing strategy, improving the bottom line

- **Comments:** The student did well. She asked a lot of good questions. Her market-sizing was clear and logical. She showed off her math and organizational skills by making the tables for both the market-sizing and the pricing issue. The student picked up on the fact that the interviewer was talking only of manufacturing costs and not all cost, therefore she was able to smoke out the additional distribution cost. Her summary was concise and articulate.

+ Yellow Stuff Chemical Company

Case 16 : Our client is a manufacturer that makes industrial cleaning solvents and pesticides. Recently, sales have been declining, mostly due to new EPA guidelines. The company has been "dumping" its old products overseas into countries that have less stringent environmental laws as well as re-engineering its products to fit the new EPA guidelines. Further evaluation of sales, both past and future, indicates that the chemical industry has and will continue to grow slowly over the next 5 to 7 years with 3% annual growth.

Management has decided to diversify. While Yellow Stuff wants to keep its chemical business intact, it also wants to enter an industry that has long-term high-growth potential. Yellow Stuff has hired us to help determine what industry or industries it should enter.

While I don't want you to come up with a list of industries, I do want you to tell me what sort of things you should be researching to determine what industry our client should diversify into.

So as I understand it, our client is a chemical manufacturer who wants to diversify outside the chemical industry into a high-growth industry.

– That's right.

And you want me to come up with a strategy on how to find the best possible match.

– Yes.

Besides diversification and profit, are there any other objectives that I should know about?

– No.

What does the company define as high-growth?

– 15% a year.

Well the first thing I'd do is obtain a list of all the industries and eliminate the ones that are growing less than 15%, or that have a potential in the next year of growing less than 15%. How much risk is Yellow Stuff willing to take?

– Medium.

Then I'd also eliminate any high-risk or volatile industries. Next I'd study the list to see if there are any synergies that we can share.

– Such as?

One example might be to look to see if there is a sister industry, where our customer list is the same. If we sell cleaning solvents to Pepsi and then we get into manufacturing aluminum, maybe we can sell Pepsi soda cans. We also have a history of marketing and selling business-to-business, so we might want to stay away from consumer products. We could look at other commonalities, such as distribution channels and sales force.

Once we narrow the list, we need to analyze the market to find out who the major players are and what, if any, the barriers to entering the market are.

– Okay, what else?

There are three ways to enter a new market: start from scratch, acquire an existing player, or do a joint venture. Depending on the industry and the barriers...

– What sort of barriers are you talking about?

Could be government regulations. If you try to start a business and your products have to get approved by the FDA or the EPA, then that could take years. In a case like that you might want to acquire an existing player. A barrier might be a stranglehold on the market: if, for example, two companies hold an extraordinarily large market share and have a habit of destroying new entries. If raw materials or supplies would be hard to come by, that would be another barrier.

– Okay.

Did I mention substitutions as a barrier?

– Summarize for me.

I'd identify all the relevant industries, analyze their markets, and determine the best way to enter that market. I'd also conduct an analysis to see if the company might not be better off just investing the money into the stock market. It may make a better return and its investment would be a lot more liquid.

- **Type of case : Entering a new market.**

- **Comments : Ninety percent of this question is irrelevant fluff. It's not about the chemical industry, it's about entering a new market. The candidate took the time to ask for the company's definition of high growth. From there, it was straight logic. Now some of you might argue that this was really a growth strategies question, but the question tells us that the client really wants to diversify, which narrows the growth strategies to one: diversification. The question then becomes one of identifying the new industry.**

✛ College Mail

Case 17 : Our client is a company named Imagitas. They have a contract with the US Postal Service to print the change of address forms that you find in your local post office. Ten years ago the change of address form was a simple green card, now the mover receives a booklet with helpful hints on how to move and coupons to stores and services that the mover will need when moving. This booklet is called "The Mover's Guide." Imagitas also sends a "Welcome Kit" to the mover's new address with coupons and information that she might find helpful in her new neighborhood. Imagitas saves the US Postal Service over $12 million dollars a year while making over $50 million in ad revenues.

One of the most active, yet hardest to reach markets is the college student. Imagitas seeks ways to segment and reach the college market. Lay out a strategic plan for Imagitas to follow, keeping in mind their objectives are to:

- **Reach students sooner**
- **Provide appropriate and attractive coupons**
- **Drive student/movers to the web site**
- **Retain mover information online**
- **Make a profit**

So basically, our client is a company that handles the change of address forms for the US Postal Service. They want us to help them segment the college market, while meeting the objectives of reaching students sooner, providing appropriate coupons, getting students to use the web site and retain information on line while making a profit.

– Basically.

Can people currently do a change of address on-line?

– That will happen soon. So you can make that assumption.

The coupons that Imagitas sends out to movers, are they from local merchants or national chains?

– National chains, although we hope to distribute local merchants soon.

I can think of five segments to this market. Heading to school for the first time, heading back to school, moving back home with their parents for the summer, moving to a new city for a summer internship and moving to a new city for their first job. The three that I'd like to focus on first are heading to school for the first time, heading back to school – each year, and moving to a new city for their first job.

– Go on.

Heading to school for the first time is a great opportunity for a very strong Mover's Guide package if sent early enough before the parents go shopping. Coupons for Linens & Things and The Gap might be good additions to the Mover's Guide.

When the student arrives on campus, the Welcome Kit can be unique with a strong mix of national and local coupons, if segmented by school or city. Coupons should be for "room stash," batteries, pizza, dry cleaners, that sort of thing.

With the group that is heading back to school I'd focus mostly on the "Welcome Kit." If Imagitas can segment by school or city then they can get a large number of local merchants as well as national chains.

Finally, there is the group that is moving to a new city for the first job. Again, this gives us a great opportunity to weigh heavy on the "Welcome Kit." This group will need everything and now has a paycheck to pay for it. National retailers like Create & Barrel and Linens & Things should jump on it.

– What you're saying is good, but how can Imagitas reach students and get them to use the web site?

College students can be reached through a variety of channels, such as strategic partnerships with universities, advertising through trade-outs, and word of mouth. Preferably, we would like to capture student data before they get on-campus. The best possible solution would be to work with university admission and housing offices to place the USPS web address in their acceptance and housing letters.

– Why would schools do this?

This would save the schools a lot of work and money in the long run. First, we should build an alliance with university mail centers. Every summer university mail centers across the country receive tons of mail for recent graduates, students away for the summer, and students who have transferred or dropped out. It's an expensive and time-consuming effort to return or worst yet, forward their mail.

In the spring, University Mail Services (UMS) usually places a postcard in the mailbox of all on-campus students urging them to notify both the USPS and the University mail services of their new address. I know that Harvard UMS keeps a database for students who have notified them, although I'd imagine the percentage of students that comply is probably pretty low. I know I get those notices every year and never remember to fill it out.

In return, University mail centers should be willing to place a "Mover's Guide" into every on-campus mailbox to try to eliminate or curtail this burden. First, it would save them the expense of printing the postcards; second, the on-line switching through the USPS site would greatly curtail their excess mail.

Through the university mail services, Admissions and Housing offices we could capture a significant percentage of the college population and retain them as they move through their different life stages. In addition, by-school segmentation makes us more attractive to local vendors.

– How else can students get the word?

Word of mouth. One cannot over emphasize "word of mouth." Word gets around fast, and now with such a large percentage of this group using email it has amplified the message and multiplied the listeners. If it is "quick and cool" it can be done.

– Can you summarize for me?

USPS and Imagitas should capture college students early, ideally before they go to college. They can do this by working in conjunction with colleges and universities by helping them reduce their excess mail load. USPS can collect the student's information in a database and have the individual update it over the Internet a month before each move. USPS can even send out an automatic email a month before the student moves prompting them to make the change on line.

Once they sign up, the student can reinitiate their move over the Internet using a PIN number, not only in college, but for the rest of their lives. USPS will promptly mail them a confirmation notice and Imagitas would mail out the mover's guide to their current address. The mover's guide will continue to have coupons for products and services to help them move. Finally, a "Welcome Kit" will be sent to the new address.

There is one more thing I'd like to add that we didn't talk about and that's the web site. Besides changing my address, it would be very helpful if I could order my phone and cable service at the same time. So maybe the web site should have links to the appropriate companies in my new area. That way, by the time I move in I'll be all set. Also, maybe there could be on-line coupons as well. I mention this because when you're moving your room's a mess and things tend to get lost. The last thing I unhook is my computer so I'll have access to the web page.

– Excellent. I'll have to remember that for my next meeting with Imagitas.

- **Type of Case: Strategy / marketing**

- **Comments: Although this is a strategy case it didn't fit neatly into one of the six strategy scenarios in the Ivy Case Method. The student was asked about how to reach a segment of which she is a part – thus she put herself in the mix and tried to figure out how to reach students like her. Her answer went into more detail than most case questions require, however, when you have a question that asks how do you reach a specific market a little more detail is required.**

+ Road to Ruin

Case 18 : A chemical company recently developed a road-surfacing compound designed to extend the life of major highways. Currently, the federal and state governments must completely dig up and replace their highways every five years. If highways are treated with this chemical, their effective life span increases to 20 years. Currently, the government spends $1,000 per mile to replace its roads. The total cost of the chemical (production and application) amounts to $50 per mile. The management of the Chemical company would like to know the following:

- **Estimate the number of miles of state and federal highways in the U.S.**
- **How should management price the product?**
- **What other issues should the company be aware of?**

Let me make sure I understand. A chemical company has developed a compound that extends the life of highways from 5 to 20 years. Currently, it costs the government $1,000 a mile to rip up a road and replace it. We can apply the compound for $50 a mile, and this $50 covers all development and application costs. Now the client wants us to estimate the number of government highway miles, price the product on a per mile basis, and determine what other issues we should be taking into consideration.

– Yes.

Besides those three items, are there any other objectives or goals I should be aware of?

– No.

How big is this chemical company?

– It's a venture-backed start-up. This is their first and only product.

Are there any other competitors or substitutions? And do we have a patent?

– No and yes, respectively.

We know the advantages of this product, but are there any disadvantages to this product like environmental concerns?

– Excellent question, but the answer is no.

Okay, let's start with the first request. To estimate the number of government highway miles I'm going to make some assumptions. First, I'm going to assume that the distance between the east and west coasts is 3,000 miles and that the distance between the northern and southern borders of the U.S. is 2,000 miles. I'm also going to assume that if you straighten out all the highways you'll have ten roads running east to west and another ten running north to south. So ten times 3,000 is 30,000 and ten times 2,000 equals 20,000 miles. Add them together and you get approximately 50,000 miles of government highways.

– Okay, I'll buy that. What's next?

We need to determine a price. There are several pricing methods that we can look at as a base and then make a determination. There is competitive pricing, but since we have no competitor this is impossible. We can look at substitutions, which is what the government is currently doing – ripping up the roads at a cost of $1,000 a mile every five years. Since this process lasts for 20 years we should use 20 years as a common denominator. I'll get back to that in a minute. And we can use cost-based pricing and stick a margin on top. Our cost is $50 per mile. If we double that to a 100 percent mark up, we'd come up with a price of $100 a mile. Finally, we can look at price-based costing. This is what the government would be willing to pay.

I mentioned the 20-year common denominator. So if you take 50,000 miles and multiply it by 4 you get 200,000 miles. Under the current plan it costs the government 200,000 times $1,000 a mile which equals - $200 million dollars. Our break-even point is 50,000 times $50, which equals $2.5 million. So our price range is $2.5 million to $200,000 million.

– That's quite a range.

I think it is time to look at some of the other factors. If the government does this it will have the construction lobby on its back, not to mention the labor unions. People will be laid off and the government will be facing unemployment issues and payments. Even though I'm assuming that this is a department of transportation decision you can bet that Congress will weigh in on the subject. So the secret is to price it so that the savings are substantial and Congress can't stop it without looking fiscally irresponsible. What if we charged them $100 million – we would be in good shape and that's half of what they pay now. They can divert the $100 million in savings to other infrastructure projects so no one gets laid off.

– So what does that breakdown to per mile?

Fifty thousand miles divided into $100 million equals - $20,000 a mile – no that's wrong it's $2,000 a mile.

– Are you sure?

Yes, $2,000 a mile. In addition, as far as cash layout goes, the government currently pays $50 million a year. Our total is $100 million. We can spread that over the length of the project, which I assumed would be two or three years.

– Okay. Thanks for coming by.

- **Type of Case: Estimate the market size, new product, and pricing.**

- **Additional Comments: This is an interesting case because it touches on so many different aspects and scenarios. The student first asked about the product, then she estimated the market size. She was smart enough not to answer the pricing question until she took the outside factors into account.**

✛ The Gas Company

Case 19 : A natural gas local distribution company (an LDC, which distributes gas locally as a monopoly) is trying to centralize its back-office functions. In the past, it has acquired other LDCs and placed them under its brand name.

Our job is to help reduce costs for the back-office functions, specifically the call center. The call center is the LDC's point of contact with its one million customers. Customers call with questions about billing, services, and emergencies. There are 150 full-time customer service associates who work in three shifts.

Recently, a new $25 million call center was built in Spearhead, Utah, because the labor costs are lower in Spearhead than in New York. Although the company has reduced operating costs from $8 million to $6.5 million, we want to reduce the costs of providing this function even further.

So our client is a natural gas local distribution company that wants us to figure out ways to reduce costs in its new phone center. Are there any other objectives that we should be aware of?

– No.

Can you give me a cost breakdown?

– Labor is 60%, toll-free phone calls are 20%, and miscellaneous items, licensing fees, training, IT, and utilities make up another 20%.

Can you give a call breakdown? I'll assume the majority of the calls are about billing.

– That's right. Billing calls make up 60% of the traffic, while 39% are calls regarding service questions, and less than 1% are emergency calls.

Okay, the number that worries me is the 60% labor cost. We need to see how we can reduce labor, possibly by automating the phone lines and making information available online. Some of the billing questions can be automated, things like how much do I owe? What address do I send my check to? Did you receive my last payment? They can all be answered by touch-tone.

But there will also be questions that can't be automated, such as not understanding a bill, as well as service calls, connecting and disconnecting the gas.

– Okay, so you want to automate some of the services as well as enhance our Web site?

Yes. I'll assume that a phone call to a human runs the company about $10 a call, while an automated call costs around $1, and a visit to the Web site, maybe 50 cents.

– You're pretty close.

What is the average length of the call?

– Five minutes total. That includes three to three and a half minutes of talking to the customer and two minutes of after-call work.

Is the after-call work computerized? Can the service rep write it up as he goes along?

– Some of the work could be done that way.

We need to do a workflow study. How does our talk time compare to the other LDCs?

– We're somewhere in the middle.

We should talk to the leaders and see what they are doing to reduce their talk time and after-call work. Do the computers regularly go down?

– Not since we moved into our new facility.

Finally, I'd like to examine the pattern of calling. When are the peak times? Is there any dead time? Can we bounce queued calls to our other phone centers? Can we use more part-time workers?

– Okay, good. We have about a minute left.

Then let me summarize. I'd try to reduce our labor costs by automating some of the calls, making more information available on the Web, staggering work shifts, using part-time workers, and having queued calls bounced to other phone centers. I'd try to reduce talk time and after-call work by having the phone rep input the work while on the line with the customer. And I'd review the information that the phone rep is recording. Is it all necessary, or are we collecting some information out of habit?

Type of case : Reducing costs.

Comment : Her focus was on reducing costs, which was exactly right. The problem wasn't so much that costs had gotten out of control, but that the company was simply looking for ways to further reduce costs. This candidate wasn't afraid to ask for a cost breakdown and to explore the savings that the Internet can create.

✛ Texas Star Markets

Case 20 : Our client is a large grocery chain throughout Texas. Their stores are concentrated in suburbs outside all the major cities in Texas; Dallas, Arlington, Fort Worth, Houston, Austin, Galveston, San Antonio, Amarillo, Corpus Christi, El Paso and Padre Island. They are looking to grow the company – but only in Texas. They feel that they have saturated the grocery market in the suburbs and have dismissed the idea of opening up stores downtown. They already have an online grocery ordering and delivery service. So, they are thinking of entering into the convenience store business. Is this a good idea? If so, how best to enter the market?

Basically, a large Texas-based grocery chain wants to explore the possibility of entering the convenience market. We need to determine if this is a good idea. And if it is, how best to enter this new market?

– That's right.

Besides the ones stated above are there any other objectives I should be aware of?

No.

Talking in broad strokes I'd like to figure out why the company wants to expand, what the current convenience store market is like, and then discuss ways to enter that market. Does that sound like a good idea?

– Possibly. I wouldn't have done it like that, but let's see how you make out.

I assume the reason or reasons Texas Star is entertaining this notion is because A) they have excess cash on hand and want to see if this is a better return on investment than a money market or other investments they've looked at. B), they want to increase their market share of the Texas in-store food business. C), there has been a decline in their existing business – maybe because of shrinking sales or higher costs. And or d) they see this as a growing market.

– Assumptions a,b & d are correct.

I know that there's plenty of competition with 7Eleven, Christy's, Dairy Mart, White Hen, The Red Apple and Utote-um, just to name a few. Can you give me any market share information?

– I can tell you that the leader is 7Eleven and that they did over $3 billion in sales last year. That includes both in-store merchandise and gasoline sales, but I don't know what their market share is.

Do you know how many stores they have?

– Over 58,000 in the US and Canada. But I don't think that's relevant.

You're right. The proper question should have been how many of those stores are in Texas and how many convenience stores are there in Texas?

– That's right, but I don't have that information.

I can't think of any barriers to entry, so I'll assume that's not a concern.

– What are the concerns?

While our grocery stores have name recognition, we need to figure out a way to capitalize on that and any other competitive advantage we might have. A convenience store is a convenience store. We'll probably be selling the same items as the 7Eleven around the corner. Why would be people come to us? I can think of three reasons, location, price or loyalty to the grocery chain.

– Okay, I like that. Explore it some more.

Well the first one was location. Which leads me to the next question – how do we plan to enter the market? We can start from scratch, buy our way in or do a strategic alliance.

– Texas Star doesn't want to do a strategic alliance.

I'd like to come back and visit this question in a minute. However, we would need to look at the real estate market and see what kinds of locations are available. We may want to see if there is a small chain of existing stores with good locations but poor management that we could take over.

– What else?

Next on the list was price. This is where I think we make our mark. People pay for convenience. Prices are high because costs are high because stores tend to buy many items in low volumes. One of our advantages is that we already buy large amounts of all the products we would sell in the store. So we have economies of scales working for us. We should be able to leverage our current value chain components.

What does that mean?

To be honest, I'm not sure.

– Let's call a time out for a second. Never use jargon or phrases that you don't understand. If you do it in an interview then I'll assume that you will do it in front of a client. It's easy for the interviewer to lose trust in a candidate, because I can't trust you in front of a client. Now it just so happens that I like you and that you are doing really well on the question, so I'm going to pretend that I didn't hear that. Continue. Where were we?

We were discussing price. If we can price our items somewhere between what we charge in our grocery stores and what our competitors charge in their convenience stores we could drive in traffic. For instance, if I buy a gallon of milk at the grocery store it costs me $2.95. If I buy that same product in a convenience store it costs me $3.95, a dollar more. If we could price it at $3.49, that's a significant enough difference where it would drive people into the store. In addition, I'm assuming that Texas Star like most large grocery stores has store-label items,

such as their own brand of peanut butter. Those items sell for significantly less than the traditional name brands. So the price difference would be even greater. We could offer all the traditional convenience store items while adding things like a salad bar and prepared gourmet meals. This could change the genetic code of convenience store retailing.

– Let's not get carried away.

Let's look at the company's resources and capabilities. We buy in large volume, we have the management team, the marketing team, trained workers, name recognition, and we have an untraditional marketing channel through our existing stores. I don't think that there would be any cannibalization of existing grocery store sales, because items would still be less expensive in the grocery store. In fact we could cross market and offer coupons to try our convenience stores.

The last thing on my list was brand loyalty. Texas Star obviously has a strong following, a commitment to Texas and I'm guessing to local communities.

– All right, summarize for me.

Texas Star is looking to expand. Their idea of getting into the convenience store market is a viable one. This market will continue to grow and there are no major barriers to entry. It will allow Texas Star to build on their name recognition and take advantage of the organization's existing resources and capabilities. They can offer lower prices and store-brand items, cross market with their grocery stores and offer new items to traditional convenience store fare.

The best way to enter the market is to look for a small chain that has good locations but bad management. Buy the chain, change the name and bring in your own management. All stores should be in close proximity to a Texas Star grocery store. If they can't find a buy-out target then they should start from scratch.

And I just want to restate that it is a combination of name recognition, location and prices that will make this idea a success.

– Okay, well that was pretty good. Now you got me thinking. Texas Star, as you can tell is always looking for new ways to increase their revenue streams. They are also considering opening an in-store bank. No other competitors in their area are currently doing it. What do we need to be thinking about?

Again, they are entering a new market. There are a number of things that they need to figure and decide. First, do they have the space in their stores or will they have to construct additional space? Also, if they do have the space we need to think about whether that space can be used more effectively. How much space is needed?

– It's the equivalent of a florist department and we already have one of those. And yes, we do have the space for this. It would take some remodeling, but nothing significant.

We need to look at who the major players are; what size market share they have; will our products or services be any different from our competitions and are there any barriers to entry.

– What would you guess?

That there's plenty of competition and that our products or services might be basic compared to our competitors. All we really have to offer them is convenience. Hopefully there will be increased traffic at the grocery stores due to the bank. But now, with ATMs, debit cards and cash back the basic services are easily covered. I'm thinking that we need to figure out how best to enter the market and determine if this makes sense.

There are three ways to enter the market. Start from scratch; buy our way in; and a joint venture. What are the costs in each of theses options? What are the potential revenue streams and how do they differ, and what is the risk associated with each?

– Do a quick cost benefit analysis for each.

Starting from scratch will be time consuming and somewhat expensive. We'd have to hire new people with experience in banking to run the organization. There might be some barriers due to federal and state banking regulations which might take some additional time. And if it fails or doesn't live up to expectations it could damage the overall Texas Star brand. On the other hand, we already have locations and our rent would be minimal. Revenues will come from bank transactions and possibly increased grocery sales. However, I'm not convinced that this is the best way.

Buying our way in would mean buying an existing bank and taking over their business. We would already have the people in place, a number of existing locations, and some brand recognition. It might be expensive. We would have to do due diligence on the entire bank and the banking industry. We might be able to sell some the branches to other banks to help reduce any debt we would incur. This would be really jumping in with both feet.

The third way would be a joint venture with an existing bank. I think this is the simplest solution and holds the least risk to profits and our brand. We would just lease space to the bank for a monthly fee. We would have to weigh the rental income against the remodeling costs.

– So what are you saying?

I would tell Texas market, that if they feel that having a bank branch in their grocery stores would result in increased traffic and maybe higher sales then they should form a joint venture with an existing bank and keep risk to a minimum and lease out the space. Starting from scratch or buying an existing player is expensive and risky. We currently know nothing about the industry and a failure could hurt the Texas Star brand.

- **Type of Case: Entering a new market(s)**

- **Comments: Besides getting into trouble for using business jargon that he did not know, the interviewee did pretty well. He laid out his strategy up front and stuck to it, but also added ways that the client could differentiate itself from the competition. He seemed to roll into the banking part of the case with a little more confidence.**

+ Longest-lasting Light Bulb

Case 21 : GE, they bring good things to life, has invented a new light bulb that never burns out. It could burn for more than 500 years and it would never blink. The director of marketing calls you into her offce and asks, "How would you price this?" What do you tell her?

Let me make sure I understand. GE has invented a light bulb that never burns out, and the marketing director wants us to help her decide on a price.

– That's correct.

Is coming up with a price the only objective? Or is there something else I should be concerned about?

– Pricing is the only objective.

Is there any competition for this product, and do we have a patent?

– We have a patent pending, and there is no other competition.

We know that the advantage is that this bulb never burns out. Are there any disadvantages to this product? Does it use the same amount of electricity?

– There are no disadvantages, except maybe price. And that's why you're here.

What did you spend on R&D?

– It cost $20 million to develop this product.

What are the costs associated with a conventional light bulb?

– It costs us $.05 to manufacture. We sell it to the distributor for $.25, the distributor sells it to the store for $.50, and the store sells it to the consumer for $.75.

And what does it cost us to manufacture the new light bulb?

– $5.00

So if we use the conventional bulb-pricing model, that would mean that the consumer would have to pay $75 for this light bulb. If we use another simple model and say that a light bulb lasts a year and that people will have this new bulb for 50 years, that's an argument for a retail price of $37.50 (50 years x $.75). Then we need to ask ourselves whether a consumer would pay $37.50 for a light bulb that never wears out. Now we're looking at price-based costing. What are people willing to pay? And is it enough to cover our costs and give us a nice profit?

The other main issue is that the more successful we are, the less successful we'll be in the future. For every eternal light bulb we sell, that's 50 or 75 conventional bulbs we won't sell in the future. In a sense, we're cannibalizing our future markets. So we have to make sure that there is enough of a margin or profit to cover us way into the future.

– Good point.

I'll tell you, I have reservations about selling to the consumer market. I just don't think the opportunity for pricing is there.

– So, what do we do, scrap the project? We've already spent over $20 million in R&D.

Not at all. We turn to the industrial market. For example, the City of Cambridge probably has 2,000 street lamps. Those bulbs cost maybe $20 and have to be changed twice a year. The real expense there isn't the cost of the bulb; it's the labor. It might take two union workers. In addition, you have to send out a truck. It probably costs the City $150 in labor costs just to change the light bulb. Now if we were to sell them this ever-lasting bulb for $400, they would make that money back in less than two years and we would make a handsome profit.

– Not bad.

Type of case : Pricing

Comments : First, the candidate looked at cost-based pricing and realized that the price was too high and that the typical consumer would not shell out $75 for a light bulb. Then he looked at price-based costing and concluded there wasn't enough of a margin built in to make it profitable. Thinking outside the outline given in the pricing case scenario, the student also realized that he would be cannibalizing his future markets. Thus, he decided that neither pricing strategy made sense for the retail market. So instead of suggesting that GE just cut its losses and walk away from the project, he went looking for alternative markets and concluded that there was great potential in the industrial market.

Because this product has yet to be released, and is without competition, the supply and demand theory doesn't work in this case.

+ eTailers

Case 22 : Our client is an e-tailer, not unlike eToys. Independent research shows that 5% of shoppers at brick and mortar retail stores make a purchase and 40% buy items at specialty stores like sporting goods shops.

The research shows that only 1.7% of their on-line visits results in a purchase. It also shows that 70 percent of their on-line shoppers who fill their carts bail out at the end without making a purchase. The President wants to know what's wrong and how we can fix it.

Our client is concerned because 70 percent of its customers, who fill up their shopping carts, bail out on their purchases right at the end. And only 1.7% of their customers makes a purchase, a percentage much lower than the traditional brick and mortar shppers.

– That's correct.

Besides identifying why people bail and coming up with a solution, are there any other objectives we need to be concerned about?

– No.

I'd like to ask some questions first about our client and then about the industry. Are we considered a specialty store?

– Yes.

Is the transaction rate at Web-based specialty retailers higher then general e-tailers?

– Yes. But I don't have the exact figures.

Is this a Web-wide problem? Do most e-tailers have a low percentage of actual purchases? What did you say it was, 1.7 percent?

– Yes. It is a Web-wide problem to a certain extent. Some sites have higher transaction rates than others. However we seem to be in the higher range of the bail rates, the 65% that bail after filling their carts has us really concerned.

First, I'd conduct an analysis of our competition. I would also benchmark other sites that have a higher transaction rate to see if their sites are friendlier, easier to navigate and more simple in structure. I'd review and compare our customer service program and maybe institute an 800 customer service number in case a customer gets lost or confused. We may even want to look into a customer service audio connection through the computer.

– All right. What's next.

Is our pricing the same as our competitors?

– Yes. Assume exactly the same.

Have we had any problems with inventory, being out of stock?

– No.

How about sending the product out in a timely manner?

– No. Our distribution system is excellent.

I'd like to figure out why people bail. We know that it is not because of our reputation, that we're well respected in the industry, we haven't had any distribution problems or bad press.

– That's right.

I've bailed once or twice myself. There could be several reasons. First, I'd like to list several reasons, address each one, then lay out a plan for solving the problem.

– Go ahead.

First is the security issue. If the Web site asks for what shoppers think is invasive personal information. If the customers don't feel comfortable submitting their credit card information on-line, if they feel that we don't have the latest cryptic technology they may bail.

– Not a concern. We only ask for basic information and we have the latest technology.

Another reason I bail is because I have questions about the quality of the product.

– Again, not a concern. We sell brand name toys and have a satisfaction guarantee.

What about our return policy?

– We provide labels and free postage for any returned item.

Sometimes I bail when I find myself asking, "Do I really need this? Can I afford it? Is it worth the price?" I guess you'd put that under customer psychology. That's hard to quantify.

– Let's skip that for now.

There may be folks who get sidetracked in the middle of a transaction. Maybe their boss walked in or their kids knocked over the fish bowl. They forget about it or decide that they don't need it. We've lost the moment so to speak. Combine this with some ISP's like AOL that time-out after ten minutes of inactivity.

– Again, that's hard to combat.

It may be hard to combat, but we have to realize that it happens and it makes up a certain percentage of the bails. Just like window and price comparison shoppers.

– So noted.

It could also be tied to some technical issues. If a customer comes over a phone line and the Web site is heavy with graphics it may take a long time going from one page to another. They can become impatient and bail.

– That's not our fault if the consumer has outdated equipment.

Sure it is. Anything that keeps them from making a purchase is our fault. Maybe we should offer them an option of taking a heavy graphic site or a text-based site.

– Very good. What else?

Next is Web design. I know that there were times when I wanted to take something out of my cart and couldn't figure out how to do it, so I either started all over again or bailed.

– All right Web design that's one. What else?

This one is related. It has to do with customer service. If I can't figure out online how to return a product then I just want someone to help me. I don't want to figure out it by reading a help button.

– You're lazy.

No, but when I want to buy something it should be a pleasant experience and I shouldn't have to work for it.

– What else?

Sticker shock. There have been times when I've come to the end of a buying trip and the numbers total up and it's more than I've expected. And then they throw on a shipping charge on top of that. I think people bail because of sticker shock. The Internet has a rep of having the lowest prices. When the prices aren't that low people become disillusioned.

– What can we do about that?

Sticker shock can be addressed by instituting a running total for the customer to see at all times, along with shipping options and charges. This way there are no surprises.

– Do you think people will buy less if they see the running totals?

There will be the possibility that the average purchase amount may fall, but in the end more people will buy offsetting any lost.

– Anything else?

Yes. We have to realize that some of the people who bail are children taking a fantasy trip through the toy store. They fill up their carts and bail at the end. Now I don't think that this is actually a bad thing. But we need to realize that x percentage of the bails are kids for whom we should develop a wish basket or toy chest.

– A wish basket?

A place where they can deposit their toys, label it with their email address and then have the parents check it out for holidays and birthdays. Kind of like registering for a wedding.

– We have a minute left.

Then I'd like to summarize. First I'd conduct an analysis of Web sites that have a lower bail rate and higher transaction rate than we do. I'd also analyze our competitors. I'll assume that we are doing this anyway. I would also try to track down the people who bailed, send them a quick on-line survey to determine why they bailed and offer them an incentive to make a purchase, like five dollars off their next purchase. Second, I'd reexamine the reasons why people bail and address the ones we could, and resign myself to the fact that there are some things we can't fix. I'd institute a place for kids to register their toys so that parents, relatives and friends can buy something they like.

▶ Type of case: Increasing sales.

▶ Comments: This isn't your typical increasing sales case. It's more of the "analyze and fix it" variety. The student was good at identifying the real concern (the 70% bail rate). He asked some good initial questions and he used his own experience to try to identify the root of the problem. Then he came up with a simple and logical strategy and added some suggestions as well.

✢ Screw Tops for Fine Wine

Case 23 : You are the owner of a small to medium-size fine winery. You're considering whether or not to switch from corks to screw tops in your current vintage. This year's wine will not be released to the general public for six years. Industry estimates are that within ten years 80 percent of all wine will have a screw top, not a cork. Should you switch over now?

The issue is whether or not to switch from cork to screw tops for the current vintage which won't be released for six years. And it looks as if the industry or at least part of the industry is switching over. Is the objective to save money?

– No.

What percentage of wines currently has screw tops?

– Are you talking retail?

Yes.

– About thirty percent.

If wines aren't for retail sale, which I take it means package stores and restaurants, then what's the other market?

– Well it's not really another market. The great wine chateaus of France and vineyards of California use screw tops in their library wines, their private collection and their test wines.

Because it's cheaper?

– No, screw tops are more reliable, they don't dry out, they don't affect the taste, they're easy to use, you don't need a cork screw, and you can reseal them. People, who truly care about wine, care about the taste and not the ceremony.

What about corks?

– Corks sometimes have mold, which affects the wine's taste. They dry out and crack if not stored properly; sometimes they crumble when you unscrew them. Now I feel as if you are trying to get me to answer the case for you.

Okay, sorry. I know now that it's not about the cost. Even though I'll assume that screw tops are less expensive because the cheaper wines use them. It's about tradition and image. When dinning out it's fun to watch the waiter at a restaurant uncork it, it makes a great sound and it's fun to smell the cork and pretend that you know what you're doing.

– Kind of like what you're doing with this case question – pretending.

(smiles) Would we have to retool our plant to switch from cork to screw tops?

– Good question, but it's not relevant because I told you cost is not an issue.

I was thinking along the lines of timing not cost. How long will it take us to retool the plant, not how much? We have three options. We can cork the entire vintage, we can screw top the entire vintage, or we can split the vintage between the two. Industry trends look as if they are headed this way, but as of today it hasn't caught on. I would want to know what the wine industry is going to do to educate the public that screw tops are better. I'd like to know what our competitors are planning to do. I'd like to do a focus group to get the reaction of wine connoisseurs and general public.

– We have no time for that. The wine has to be bottled soon and we need to place the order now. What's it going to be, yes or no?

If I had to decide today then I'd stay with the corks. The cork system has worked for thousands of years. I think that there is a higher risk bottling our best vintage with screw tops then not having it catch on. I know that you said that the people who care more about the taste than ceremony would choose screw top over cork, taste over image, but I think most people aren't that sophisticated.

– Isn't there the option of holding the wine an extra year or two until screw tops are accepted in fine wine? It's not going to go bad; in fact it might even be more valuable. The least we could have done is split it and sell the corks in six years and hold on to the screw tops longer if need be.

Maybe a split. How expensive is this wine? Until you get James Bond unscrewing a bottle of Margeaux or champagne on the silver screen I would wager that it is not going to fly with the general public – unless the industry as a whole does it together. Until they all make the switch on a certain date in time.

Okay, now pretend that you are advising the National Wine Association on how to get the public to switch from corks to screw tops.

It's important that we have a consensus in the industry, not only domestically but, internationally as well. France, Germany, Australia, and Chile should all sign on. Certainly an industry media campaign along the lines of "Got Milk" would be in order. It's not each individual vineyard going it alone. I'd help the smaller vineyards prepare for the switch, maybe even make it a countdown situation – 2005 the year of the screw top. I'd make it a big deal and not try to quietly switch over. Not only would I try to get stories on the news and in the newspaper, I'd try to get screw tops on television shows and in the movies. And yes, I'd try to get James Bond to unscrew a bottle of champagne on screen – I'm sure his screenwriters can come up with a catchy little sexual quip to make it all worth while. After all he did switch from an Astin Martin to a BMW.

– I guess this is where I tell you to stick a cork in it.

Isn't that what James Bond said to Dr. Christmas Jones in "The World is Not Enough."

– No, your answer was not enough. Thanks for coming by.

- **Type of Case:** Strategy / marketing

- **Comments:** It wasn't the fact that the student asked a lot of questions, it was the type of questions that he asked. He would have been better off making assumptions about the advantages and disadvantages of screw tops and corks than asking for it since that information is so critical to the question. He did roll with the punches; however, I don't think that the interviewer had much of a sense of humor. The student didn't back down when the interviewer questioned his decision about using corks, but he compromised a little. His first reference to James Bond was powerful, but he took the Bond chatter too far.

✛ Fuel Efficiency

Case 24 : Our client is a large auto manufacturer who is thinking about making a device that will increase fuel efficiency in your car by 20 percent. What is the market for this product? What should it be priced at?

We have a large automaker that is thinking about making a device that will increase fuel efficiency in your car by 20 percent. They want to know what the market is and how much should they charge. Are those the only two objectives that I should be aware of?

– Objectives? Yes.

I have some questions. You said "thinking of making a device." Does that mean they have the technology? Have they already done the research?

– Yes. It's possible. The research is done and the prototype has been made and tested.

You also said 20 percent. So that means my SUV which now gets 20 miles to the gallon will soon get 24 miles to the gallon.

– Yes, that's what 20 percent means.

What are the disadvantages of this product? Are there environmental concerns, like increased emissions? Does the car lose much of its power?

– There is approximately a 5 percent loss of power. That is the only disadvantage.

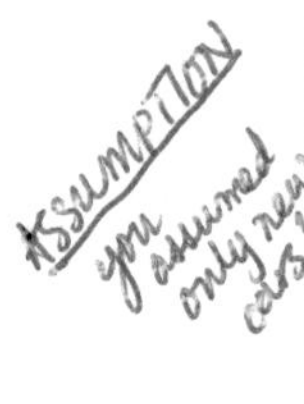

Will this device be sold in the aftermarket or will it only be offered on new cars? Will it be an option on new cars or a standard item?

– All of the above. It will work on any car manufactured after 1997.

Do they have a patent?

– No. This is has been fairly common knowledge in the auto industry. They could have made this device back in the early seventies when we had gas lines.

Why didn't they?

– Why do you think?

Too expensive? I'm guessing that with new technology and with the price of gas increasing they think now is the time. So before I determine the market size I'd like to figure out the price. Do we know what it will cost them to produce this item?

– Twenty dollars.

Does that include R&D expense? Building the plant?

– When we figure in everything it runs $25 a unit.

Is it easy to install?

> – Yes. We estimate that the average garage will charge $75 to install this device in the aftermarket.

Okay. Let's look at the pricing strategies. I can't think if there is anything else out there like this.

> – Not really.

But since this technology is common to the industry, if we're successful then I can imagine other firms jumping in rather quickly, especially in Europe where the price of gas is much higher.

> – Absolutely. We can talk about that later if there's time. Let's just concentrate on the US market. You were looking at pricing, let's stick with that for now.

Competitive analysis – we have nothing to compare it to. That leaves cost –based pricing and price-based costing. Cost-based pricing, if it costs us $25 and we add a 50 percent margin on that means we would sell it to the distributors for $37.50, the distributors would probably sell it to the auto parts store or garages for $50, who would sell it to the customer for $75. So in the end it would cost the consumer for the device and to have it installed - $150 in the after-market.

Let's figure that the average gallon of gas is $1.50 and the consumer gets 20 miles to the gallon. The tank holds 20 gallons. It costs $30 to fill the tank. That means currently I can drive 400 miles on a tank of gas. So with this new device I can drive 480 miles on a tank of gas. So 80 miles divided by 20 miles a gallon equals a savings of 4 gallons times $1.50, which comes to $6 a tank. If the average person drives 15,000 miles per year, we divide 15,000 by 480 per tank, which equals around 30 tanks. We're saving $6 per tank times 30 tanks equals a savings of around $180, more than enough to cover the cost of the new device. About a one-year pay-back.

Another way to look at it is $1.50 per gallon divided by 20 miles to the gallon equals 7 cents per mile. With this device we have $1.50 a gallon divided by 24 miles to the gallon equals 6 cents per mile. So we are saving a penny a mile. If the average person drives 15,000 miles a year, which equals $150 in savings. Basically ii would take the average person a year to get his money back. Half that time, if he installs it himself.

The more expensive cars usually get less mileage and we could probably charge more. The less expensive cars, let's say one that gets 30 mpg would change to 36 mpg. I think this group would be less willing to pay for a few extra miles especially if it takes them a year to pay it off. You may want to market it to SUV drivers who are looking for better gas mileage and can afford the device. I would seek environmental organizations to help tout the device. So for the aftermarket I think our pricing is in line at $37.50, maybe we could even charge $40.

If competitors jump into the market, we'll have to review the cost structure and look at manufacturing this device in Mexico or Asia. One advantage that we would have is economies of scale. If we are producing this device for all our new cars then we'll have a pretty solid volume, especially if we can produce it for other OEMs. Still a competitor who uses non-union labor and cheaper material might have a significant advantage in the aftermarket.

– How do you compete with that?

One, you market the quality of the part and two; you require all dealerships to use genuine parts.

How do you think the oil companies will react?

They're not going to be happy, but they will look pretty bad if they try to block the development and manufacturing of such a device. They'll be painted as almost unpatriotic. Instead, they will raise the price of gasoline two cents a gallon, no one will notice and they'll make a killing.

– Your next interview with ExxonMobil?

No, no. I just want to do consulting.

Type of Case: Strategy and pricing.

Comments: His math was good and he approached the problem two different ways to see where his cost-based pricing answers crossed, however he never discussed price-based costing or how much each unit will add to the cost of a new car.

+ New York Opera

Case 25 : Our client is the New York City Opera. They want to develop a growth strategy for the next five years. What would you advise them to look at, and what are your recommendations for growth?

The New York City Opera wants us to develop a growth strategy for the next five years.

– That's right.

Besides developing this five-year strategy are there any other objectives?

– No.

So I don't need to look at increasing sales, reducing costs or increasing profits?

– Those are all key ingredients to growth, are they not?

Yes, I guess they are. I was just trying to determine the direction of the question. I'd like to ask a few questions. Is the industry growing?

– No, down seven percent last year.

How are we fairing compared to the industry?

– Better, but not much. Our growth rate last year was two percent.

Who are our competitors and how much market share does each one have?

– Who do you think our competition is?

It's anyone or anything that competes for the leisure dollar. It could be as wide spread as a restaurant, a hockey game, events at Lincoln Center, or a trip to the Hamptons. But it is also other opera companies in New York. I'm not sure how many opera companies there are in New York.

– There're about four. The biggest is the Metropolitan Opera. Can you name any operas?

Sure. There's Tommy and Figaro. Oh, and The Barber of Seville.

– Okay. That helps me put your answer in perspective. So what do you do?

The first thing I would do is a competitive analysis. I would not only look at the other four New York opera companies, but those in other major US cities and maybe London and Paris.

– What would you analyze?

Everything. Revenues and revenue streams, ticket distribution outlets, fixed costs, marginal costs, production costs, season schedule, ticket prices, the names and types of operas produced, marquee names in each production, marketing campaigns and other uses for the venue.

– That's quite a list. After you did the analysis what would you do?

I'd take the best practices and see if it makes sense to incorporate any of those practices at the New York City Opera.

– You mentioned revenue streams. What do you think the revenue streams are currently?

Ticket sales, sales of programs, drinks during intermission, and merchandise like CD's, t-shirts – that sort of thing. And I think fundraising is an important revenue stream as well.

– How would you increase revenues?

Three ways. We can look at increasing ticket prices; increasing our marketing campaign to get more people to come to the opera, and then once they're there get them to spend more money.

– Can you think of additional revenue streams?

Maybe holding lectures and panels or possibly giving lessons?

– We're not offering singing lessons. What else?

I'll assume that an opera does not perform 365 days a year and that there are often stretches of time when the venue is open or in preproduction. Every night that the opera house sits empty we're losing money. So why not hold other events in the venue, specifically musical events. I mean the acoustics have to be unbelievable don't you think?

– I would imagine. Okay, good. You also mentioned ticket distribution.

Yes. I'd check to see if you can buy tickets over the web and at other ticket outlets. See if we can come up with a few additional and maybe untraditional outlets or distribution channels. I'll assume that they have discounts for season ticket holders, large groups, students and senior citizens.

– That's correct.

I think schools are a good place to educate future opera fans. We have to rebuild the audience. Get the next generation interested in opera.

– The next area you mentioned was costs. I don't want to spend too much time on this, but I'll assume that you'll work hard to reduce all our costs.

Yes.

– To be honest with you, your answer isn't going where I want it to go. I feel like we're getting too bogged down in details. The question was about growth strategy. Unless you have more to say about growth strategies we'll end this interview right now.

Well, we've talked about increasing sales by bringing in a big name singer, adding new distribution channels for tickets and merchandise sales as well as possible new revenue streams. We talked about increasing the product line and the diversity of that product line. That could

mean new merchandise or more operas, but I think it means different shows, concerts or maybe standup comics revues. Anything that fills the opera house on nights when there is no performance. A third strategy, that doesn't apply, but I thought I would mention is acquiring the competition, maybe buying one of the smaller opera companies. But it doesn't sound like we have a lot of extra cash on hand and what we do have can be better allocated toward driving more people in our door.

– That was a nice summation, but there was nothing new there.

One last thing. This summer I worked for a mutual fund company and what we discovered is that 95 percent of the business came from 5 percent of the customer base. This company wasn't fully taking advantage of the opportunities to grow through its existing customer base. Up until this summer they never differentiated between customers who represented real profits and customers that only represented costs.

– This is good, continue.

They found that over one-third of the money spent on marketing and customer service was wasted on efforts to acquire new customers who cost us more than we made. In some cases we were marketing toward our established customers when that money could have been better spent.

– So what are you telling me?

We should focus the company on bringing in new and profitable customers. That may mean changing the way we currently and traditionally market. It means developing better relationships with our profitable customers. And finally it means abandoning those customers that cause us to lose money.

– I think that theory applies to a mutual fund company better than an opera company, but I'll give you points for trying.

Type of Case: Growth strategies.

Comments: Her answer was all over the place. Parts of it were very strong, others weren't. She went off on a tangent and got herself into trouble. The other thing is that she never really came up with anything extraordinary. Everything she mentioned had been tried before. The last bit about growing through existing customers and weeding out the dogs was interesting if not totally relevant.

Editor's note: Many firms have a version of this question. They could ask about a music school, a museum or a symphony.

✛ High-Speed Train

Case 26 : Our client wants to open high-speed train service from Toronto to Montreal. Is this a good idea?

Our client has hired us to determine if opening a high-speed train service between Toronto and Montreal is feasible.

– That's right.

I'll assume his objective is profits.

– Profits and ego. He wants to be the next Richard Branson.

Does the client own any other trainlines, airlines, ships, hotels or travel agencies?

– He owns a couple of hotels.

Is there train service currently between those two cities?

– Yes, but it takes 3 hours compared to the 1 hour and 15 minutes that this new train will take.

I'll also assume that there is a highway as well as air service.

– That's a fair assumption.

How long does it take to drive?

– Between 3 and 4 hours depending on traffic.

And to fly?

– One hour.

What is the cost of flying?

– Roundtrip is $500.

What would be the cost of taking the train?

– We don't know yet. That's one reason why you're here.

Well first I'd like to look at the competition, that being the airlines. We know that it costs a person $500 to fly round trip. Would it be fair to assume that most passengers are business travelers?

– Yes. I can tell you that everyday approximately 5,000 people travel back and forth between Toronto and Montreal. On weekends it drops to 1,000 passengers a day.

Is that 5,000 passengers each way?

– Yes.

Just by plane?

– No. A large percentage is by plane.

How frequent are the flights and how many passengers do they hold?

– There are 40 one-way flights a day. They run every half an hour during the peak hours – early morning and early evening. During the slow periods flights run once an hour. The planes hold 100 passengers.

That's 4,000 passengers. You said they're mostly business travelers. I'll assume that the three most important things to the business traveler are speed, which also takes into account the number of delays, frequency and price. Other concerns might be cleanliness and service.

– That's exactly right.

Let me recap the plane situation. There are 40 roundtrip flights a day. They run every half an hour during peak times and every hour during off peak. They carry 4,000 business travelers every weekday. The cost is $500 for a round-trip ticket. How long does it take to get from the airport to the city?

– Half an hour, depending on traffic.

And where would the train station be located?

– Right in the city.

Okay, let's look at the train. Does the track already exist?

– No. You'd have to build it.

How expensive is that? You'd have buy and lay the track. Probably pay big bucks for property rights, that is to allow the track passage through private property.

– The total cost of laying the track is $1 billion with $5 million a year for maintenance costs.

Let's look at some of the other costs. You'd have labor, both on-board and station help. There would be advertising costs, fuel costs, the costs of purchasing train engines and passenger cars, insurance ...

– To save time, let's just say that the cost per trip is $50,000. And that you're planning 20 trips per day.

That's a million dollars a day. How many passengers can we hold?

– As many as a 1,000 per trip.

Have we done any surveys to see if business travelers would even take the train?

– Yes. Seventy-five percent of the people surveyed said that they would take the train.

At what price?

– A price equal to or less than the airlines are charging.

If 75 percent of the people surveyed said that they'd take the train, then we can probably count on half of that. Let's say that we captured 40 percent of the market, keeping in mind that it will take six months to a year to build up to that. So 40 percent of 4,000 passengers equals – 10 percent is 400 so 40 percent is 1,600 passengers a day.

If we charge $500 for a roundtrip and transport 1,600 passengers a day that would bring in revenues of $800,000. That means we'd be losing $200,000 a day even after six months of marketing expense. So we need at least 2,000 passengers a day just to break even and that doesn't take into account the $1 billion in infrastructure costs.

In short, unless we can significantly increase the number of daily passengers, raise ticket prices, or reduce our costs I'd have to advise against it.

- **Type of Case: Entering a new market.**
- **Comments: The student asked a lot of good questions. He used logic and numbers to prove his point.**

+ Bull Moose Financial Services

Case 27 : Bull Moose is a large financial services company with $98 billion under management. It has 20 different mutual funds and a brokerage company. Customers receive a statement for each individual mutual fund as well as one for their brokerage activities. So if you own four mutual funds and a brokerage account, you get five separate statements and often multiple duplicate mailings for cross products.

Another problem Bull Moose has is that its customer service phone reps can't tell what the client's total investment is in Bull Moose products. The client may have $1 million in one fund and only $2,500 in another. So a million-dollar customer may get treated like a $2,500 customer. How do we ensure that the heavy hitters (big investors) get treated like royalty when they call into Bull Moose Investments?

So Bull Moose, a large financial services company, wants to improve customer service to its large investors.

– Yes.

Besides treating its customers like royalty, are there any other objectives I should know about?

– Well, we want to keep costs down as well.

Are our competitors having the same problems?

– We can benchmark our competitors, but I want you to come up with solutions–not just copy our competitors.

Is Bull Moose a public company?

– No, it's privately held.

Okay, so we need to come up with a way to increase efficiency while making our customers feel like royalty.

– Yes.

The first thing I would do is make an investment in technology. Bull Moose is a privately held company so we can take a hit to the bottom line and Wall Street won't freak out. I would consolidate all those accounts under one account number, maybe a master account number for both monthly statements and customer service reps. That way the customers can see all their assets on one statement. We would mail only one statement instead of five, and we would also eliminate the duplicate mailings.

How many customers does Bull Moose have, and what is the average number of accounts?

– One million customers with an average of two accounts each.

So that is a savings of at least one million mailings, times four for quarterly statements, times the price of a stamp. Not to mention all the savings on cross-mailing. I also think it's important

that the phone reps have that same information, not only so they can treat a million-dollar customer like a million dollars, but also so they can service all customers better.

– Anything else?

Yes. You might want to code your customers. Break them down into groups such as platinum, gold, silver, bronze, and charcoal. Give the platinum customers an 800 number that takes priority over all calls and is picked up on one ring by a customer service rep dedicated to platinum customers. How big would this platinum group be?

– It depends on the criteria. But it's safe to say that five percent of the customers do 95% of the business.

So 5% of one million is 50,000 customers. I'm going to assume that customers call in for three major reasons–to place a trade, complain, or get account information. Does the same rep handle all these functions?

– Yes.

You may want to break it up and have two separate lines, one dedicated to trading. You're probably spending too much money paying traders to handle customer complaints when they should be trading. You could hire recent college grads to handle the complaints. I'd also allow the customers to view all their accounts online. This could reduce the number of overall service calls. And if Bull Moose doesn't already do online trading, they may want to look into it. I think I read that an online transaction is about one-tenth the cost of a phone call. You could even have an option where statements could be emailed to the client instead of going through the U.S. mail.

– All right, anything else?

Well, to summarize, I'd recommend an investment in technology that would allow customers to see a consolidated statement, and phone reps to view all of the accounts that a customer has with Bull Moose. I would code those customers so that the five percent get fast service with separate phone lines. You could print the new numbers right on the statements. As far as reducing costs, we'd save money on the mailing of statements and cross-marketing pieces. We'd also save money by hiring recent college grads to handle the customer complaint calls and letting our traders focus on trading. I would also try to get our customers to use the Internet to handle a lot of their needs. This would reduce our costs overall and allow us to give better service to all our customers.

– Great.

- **Type of Case : Reducing costs.**
- **Comments : In this case, it wasn't so much that costs have been out of control; the problem really stemmed from a customer service problem. Here, we were able to kill two birds with one stone: improve service and reduce costs.**

+ Getting into Diapers

Case 28 : DuPont has just invented a lightweight, super-absorbent, biodegradable material that would be perfect for disposable diapers. What should they do with it?

DuPont has developed a new material that would be great for disposable diapers and they want to know how best to take advantage of this product.

– Yes.

One objective is to figure out what to do with this material. Any other objectives?

– Yes, make a handsome profit. But first, I'd like you to figure out the size of the disposable diaper market.

Okay. I'm going to make some assumptions. I'll assume that the population of the U.S. is 280 million, and that the life expectancy of an average American is 80 years. I'm also going to assume that there are even numbers of people in each age group. So that means that there are the exact same number of 3-year-olds as 73-year-olds. So you divide 280 million by 80 and you get 3.5 million people per age group. Children wear diapers from age zero to three, so that's 10.5 million children. Let's round it down to 10 million children. I'm going to assume that 80% of the children wear disposable diapers, so that's eight million kids times five diapers a day equals 40 million diapers a day. Multiply that by 365 days and you get 14.6 billion diapers times, I don't know, say, $1 a diaper. So the market is $14.6 billion a year.

– So now we know the market size. What's next?

We look at the market and see who the major players are, what kind of market share each has, and what the pricing differentials are. I know P&G has a large part of that market and I know that there are a number of generic brands as well. The competition is tough, but I can't think of any barriers that would really stop us.

– So you think we should get into the diaper business?

Yes, but we need to figure what part of the business. When I asked you if there were any other objectives or goals, you said profit. What you didn't say was to become a major player in the consumer diapers market. So that means that there are several ways we can enter. I'd like to list them, then look at the advantages and disadvantages of each.

We can start up our own diaper company, form a joint venture, buy a smaller player and substitute our product for theirs, or manufacturer the diapers and license them to a number of companies.

First, let's look at starting our own company. We have name recognition but not in that industry. We would have to set up a manufacturing plant; hire a management team, marketing team, and sales force; and establish distribution channels. Time consuming and expensive, but doable.

Second, we can form a joint venture with an established diaper company. The advantages there are that the company would already have everything in place as far as name recognition, management team, sales force, and distribution channels. But we might find this limiting. Depending on the deal, we might only be able to manufacture for them.

Third, we can buy a diaper company and substitute our product for theirs. This has merit for all the same reasons the joint venture has. We need to ask ourselves if we really want to manufacture and market diapers or just manufacture them.

The fourth option was to license our product to a variety of companies. If our technology is superior to the existing product, then let's get multiple companies on board and let their marketing experts fight it out.

– Good. So which one would you choose?

With just the information I have so far, I'd venture to say the last option, manufacture and license the rights. Become a supplier and do what DuPont does best–manufacture.

We could even go to the different diaper companies and get pre-orders to ensure that the market is there and our pricing is in line.

- **Type of case : Market sizing and entering a new market.**
- **Comments : At first some might think this to be a developing a new product question, and they could probably make a decent case out of it. But the question really asks, "What should they do with it?" That implies that the product has already been developed and the company is searching for the best way to exploit this new technology; thus, this is an entering a new market case.**

What impressed the interviewer here was the fact that he picked up on what the interviewer didn't say and built on that. That's an extraordinary example of great listening—the best skill a consultant can have.

+ eOfficemanager

Case 29 : We want to start a new Web-based company that would lend support and offer advice to office managers everywhere. What sort of services should we offer? What are the potential revenue streams? How would you get started?

Let me make sure I understand. Our client wants to start a new Web-based business focusing on the common needs of office managers.

– That's right.

Besides starting a new and successful business, are there any other objectives I should be aware of?

– Just the usual: build a successful business, make a ton of dough, and fulfill a need.

What can you tell me briefly about the company, industry, and competition?

– The company was started by three co-founders. Two have experience as office managers; the other has extensive Web experience. Internet services is the industry and it is exploding; however, our competition is somewhat limited at this point. There is one other Web site that would directly compete with us. There are other sites that are geared toward office managers, but strictly focus on selling.

This is a combination of starting a new business and entering a new market. First, the market is easy to enter. There are no real barriers, except start-up capital. We've already decided that we will start from scratch, but we might want to come back and revisit the idea of doing a strategic alliance once we've identified what services we are offering. What services are we offering?

– You tell me.

The first thing I'd do is go out and interview as many office managers as I could and find out what their needs are. What we might find is that office managers want information and advice. Office managers work and function alone. They have no true colleagues in the company. They need somewhere to go, someone to talk to, someone to discuss their problems and exchange ideas and information with. I'd try to build a community aspect to the site. I'd try to determine the demographics of this group and gear my site towards its needs and problems.

We would research and/or provide links to sites that could answer such questions as identifying which copier to buy, how much to pay a temp or new employee, what the office travel policy should be, and other human resource-related issues. We could have a chat room, do opinion polls, send out an email newsletter, and maybe write a book. The other thing we could do is form an association of office managers and allow them to get greater discounts on office furniture and supplies. Once the office manager association is formed, we could hold a convention and make money from vendors and on admission fees. It would also make us a leader in the office manager industry.

– Okay, good.

Now that we know what services we could offer, let's revisit the idea of a strategic alliance. A company like Staples or Office Depot would be a good partner, because they don't just sell one item, like copiers. So we could make independent recommendations and not feel as though we had to recommend a particular copier because our sponsor makes it. The other advantage of an alliance with Staples would be that they could send us thousands of members by linking our site to theirs. We could offer our members a greater discount at Staples.

– You've done a good job covering services and you have touched on revenues. Just clarify for me what our revenue streams would be.

Ad sales, Web links, membership fees from the association, conference fees from attendees and vendors.

– How would you get started? The three partners are all throwing in $50,000 each.

First, I'd spend a great deal of time developing our Web site. Next, I'd form an advisory board. Maybe place an executive from Staples on the board, maybe a business school professor. I'd take a couple of months to research office products and salary information as well as human resource information. I'd put together a benefits package for our association members. It could include a discount at Staples, subscription discounts to certain periodicals, travel discounts–the possibilities are endless.

I'd devise a marketing and PR campaign not only to draw attention to our Web site, but also to draw attention to office managers, the unsung heroes. For the most part, office managers are under-appreciated. Our site will make them feel special.

And I'd be thinking about raising additional funds. Our overhead could be low at first because you could work out of someone's home, but once we were up and running, we'd need some space.

– Okay, good.

Type of Case : Starting a new business.

Comments : The strength of her answer was that she was willing to go to the customers to find out what they want, instead of assuming what they need. Also, she emphasized the importance of the community aspect of this Web site. She correctly identified some of the problems office managers have and thought of some services they would need.

+ WIVY FM Radio

Case 30 : Our client is the owner of a small East Coast FM radio station, WIVY. CBS-owned Infinity Broadcasting, the number three radio station owner with 160 stations and six of the country's top 10 stations, has been after him to sell. Infinity Broadcasting offered him a good price, but he has turned it down. He's making a tiny profit, but needs to do better if he is to survive. He's had to lower the cost of his on-air ads to compete with other stations. He's afraid to cut into his music with more ads because he's afraid of hurting his ratings, thus forcing his ad rates even lower. What should he do?

Approach 1 : We have a radio station that's not doing well. It's had to lower the price of its on-air ads to compete with other stations. And the station is afraid to increase the number of ads because it's afraid of losing listeners?

– Yes.

So is his objective survival?

– That's one objective. But I think he wants to thrive, not just survive.

So he needs to turn the station around by increasing ad sales, reducing costs, and making a bigger profit?

– Are you asking me or telling me?

Let me ask you this: What format does his station play?

– Classic rock and roll. Nothing too heavy.

How many other stations in that market have a similar format?

– Three.

Has he investigated other formats?

– All the popular formats have three or four stations vying for listeners. The only format that is open is country and western. And he's not interested in that.

Why is his station doing so poorly?

– You tell me.

I'll assume that it's because he can't afford to hire a big name DJ or to have on-air contests.

– True.

How are his competitors doing?

– Fine. Their market share is higher. Our station is basically at the bottom of the ratings barrel.

Do large corporations own his competitors?

– Yes.

What about his revenue streams? I'm assuming ad sales is his major source.

– For the sake of this question, assume that it's his only source.

He is probably having a hard time competing with the other stations because they have a bigger sales force and can offer a discounted package of national ads that covers all their stations.

– Safe assumption.

And you said that he was at his maximum as far as number of on-air ads.

– I don't remember saying that, but yes, he's filled all his ad spots. The problem is that he had to lower the price to get those ads.

Let's look at his costs...

– His costs have already been looked at. Everything has been cut to the bone.

Okay, so if costs have been reduced as much as possible and ad sales are maxed, then we need to think of a way to get our ratings up so we can increase the price of our ads.

– What do you propose?

He can try to raise some money so he can steal the top DJ, and then promote the hell out of it. Or he can offer the top DJ an equity piece of the station in return for coming over and bringing her audience. Either way he is going to lose some ownership.

But if he tries that and fails, and eventually sells the station, then he has to split the money from CBS with the DJ.

– Yes. That's right. So what should we tell him to do?

It's clear that he can't go on the way he has been. He's got to do something. Something dramatic. I would advise him to go after the number one DJ in the city, offer her a piece of the station at a price, then use that money to hire a PR firm to promote the new DJ. I would try to find an outside sales group to sell his ads on a commission basis; that way you're reducing his labor and benefit costs.

– You wouldn't tell him to sell the station?

If he wanted to sell it, he would have sold it.

– Okay, thanks.

Type of Case : Increasing the bottom line.

Comments : This candidate went the traditional route of exploring ways to reduce costs and increase sales and/or audience. It was a straightforward approach. For a more creative approach, read on....

Approach 2 : Okay, our client is an owner of a small FM radio station. His profits are tiny. He's reluctant to sell more ads because he's afraid his listener ratings will go down, forcing him to lower his rates even further. CBS wants to buy him out and they are offering him a fair price. He's come to us for advice.

– That's right.

Why won't he sell?

– Radio is all he knows.

What format does his station play?

– Rock and roll. Nothing too heavy. Classics from the 80s and 90s.

Has he recently changed formats?

– No.

Are there other stations that play a similar format?

– Yes, three others.

I would investigate other formats.

– All the popular formats have three or four stations vying for listeners. The only format that is open is country and western, and he's not interested in that.

Do large corporations own his competitors?

– Yes.

Sometimes we talk about barriers to entering a new market, but there are times when there are barriers to staying in a market.

– What do you mean?

His competitors are all well-financed. They probably have a team of eager salespeople that can sell ads nationally as well as locally. Much of their back-of-the-house operations are consolidated, and thus their overhead is much lower. They have more money to throw at promotions and giveaways and can therefore attract more listeners.

– That's all true, so what can we do about it?

If his objective is to stay in radio...

– CBS doesn't want him around. They don't want him running the station under their ownership. In fact, you can assume that none of the new owners would want him or any of his people around. Nothing against him, they just like to bring in their own people.

I can think of two options. The first is to partner with the number one DJ in town. Offer the DJ a piece of equity in the station. He can bring over his listeners and it would create a lot of press. Maybe go out and raise some additional capital from private investors based on the strength of this new DJ and pump some excitement into the station.

– Okay, that's one solution. What else?

The second idea needs to be researched a little more, but here goes. I'm going to make the assumption that many stations across the country struggle with late-night airtime, from 12 a.m. to 5 a.m. Listeners are far fewer, but they still have to pay an on-air personality. Fair assumption?

– Fair assumption.

Cut a deal with CBS. You sell them the station. In return, we get our great price, plus the late-night air rights to *The Howard Stern Show* archives and the late-night air rights to the *Late Night with David Letterman* archives. We syndicate a late-night program that draws from those two sources, and the CBS radio network becomes our biggest customer.

– Two good options, which one do you pick?

We don't pick. We just lay out the options for the client and allow him to decide.

– All right.

Comments : As you can see, not every case has to follow one of the scenarios. Knowing what questions to ask and being creative helps tremendously. If I were the interviewer, I would have favored this second approach simply for its creativity.

These are good cases in which the general information might be outdated, but the structure is classic. They are good practice. It makes sense to read as many cases as possible to build your own case archive in the back of your brain.

✛ AOL

AOL wants to increase its membership. It is thinking of giving a computer away with each new account that signs a three-year service contract. Is this a good idea?

So AOL wants to increase its membership and is investigating whether it should give away a computer to attract more subscribers.

– Yes.

One objective is to increase its membership. Are there any other objectives that I should be concerned about?

– Yes, profits.

How many subscribers does AOL currently have?

– As of the end of 2000 they had 25,000,000.

How many new subscribers did they get last year?

– Approximately five million new subscribers.

Five million? That's a 20% increase. What kind of percentage increase are they looking for?

– They want to increase 40 percent every year. In 1998 they went from 10.7 million subscribers to approximately 15 million, that's 40%. In 1999 they went from 15 million subscribers to 20 million. That was a 33%.

So they are peaking out at around 5 million new subscribers each year.

– Right, and as the subscriber base goes up that five million becomes a smaller percentage.

And now they want to give away a computer to entice new subscribers?

– Yes.

How much is AOL's monthly subscriber fee?

– Figure twenty dollars.

I'd like to look at the economics behind this decision. Is AOL thinking new computers, refurbished computers or Home Internet Appliances?

– You tell me.

Let's say that a computer manufacturer will sell AOL a new computer for $600, they can buy a refurbished computer for $400 or buy a HIA for $300. If their mission is to get more people on the Internet, then they might want to look at the HIA. But let's take a minute to think about who would take advantage of this offer. It seems like the elderly are going online as well as the less educated and lower income families. I think each of those groups would take advantage of this offer. The other thing is that this would probably be a first computer for those groups. Others to take advantage of this would be middle-income families looking for a second computer, possibly one to send off to college with their kid. Wait, let me shift directions for a second.

If there are 25 million subscribers and AOL wants to increase that by 40 percent we're talking 10 million new accounts – that's almost double what they're usually bringing in. That's around 4 percent of the U.S. population or 10 percent of the US households. The other issue to think about is where are they going to get 10 million new computers or even HIAs? We also need to realize that they are going to buy and give away 10 million Internet devices when 5 million people would have signed up anyway.

– Assume that our projections show that if we ran the ad campaign with new computers we could sign up 10 million new accounts. If we used refurbished computers we'd sign up 6 million new accounts and if we offered HIAs 8 million new accounts.

Let's assume that they can get their hands on 10 million new computers and that they can buy them for $600 a piece. That's $6 billion. It would probably cost you $200 million in shipping and handling as well. The revenues from this will be $20 a month times 36 months times 10 million. That's $7,200,000,000. That's a profit of $1 billion. If they didn't make this offer and increased their subscriber base by 5 million – like in years past their profit would be 5 million times $720 which equals $3.6 billion. The numbers would suggest that we not do it.

– What about the others, the refurbished or the HIAs?

For the refurbished you said 6 million at $400 each which is $2.4 billion, not including the shipping costs. The revenues would be 6 million times 720 around $4.3, which means a profit of $1.9 billion, which is still below the $3.6 billion. Besides finding 6 million refurbished computers would be a nightmare.

– And the HIAs?

HIAs at $300 times 8 million is $2.4 billion in expenses plus we'll assume $100 million in shipping charges. So that's $2.5 billion. Now our revenues would run $720 times 8 million. Let's see that's approximately $5.7 billion. The balance is $3.2 billion. Again, 400 million below what we could bring in if we stick with the current marketing plan.

Besides, if AOL is giving away computers or HIAs the manufacturers will probably take some heat from the retail stores because it's cutting into their market and supply would be limited. I don't even know if they can make 10 million HIAs a year. If they are running full capacity and have to run extra shifts while paying overtime the price of the computers or HIAs is going to rise significantly. The last thing you want is to promise 10 million new computers and then not to be able to deliver on that promise.

– So what would you tell the marketing department of AOL?

First, I might convey to them that their goal of getting 10 million new accounts is very ambitious. I would tell them stick with the current marketing plan or maybe explore ways to bundle AOL with the new computers or HIAs through the manufacturing side. I'd tell AOL that they might consider raising the price of their service a dollar per month. That would bring in additional income regardless of the number of new customers they sign up. You mentioned that their objective was twofold, increasing membership and increasing profits. This additional income would go straight to the bottom line.

– Aren't you concerned that AOL will lose a large number of customers if it raises its monthly fee?

No, it's easy to get tied into AOL. AOL has a lot of "sticky" features that keep customers. I have my email, I have my address book. Besides, I would imagine AOL's competitors will raise their prices as well.

– Interesting. Besides that question, have you ever failed at anything?

(Chuckle) Of course. But before I talk about a failure, where did I go wrong on the question?

– You didn't. I just wanted to see if you could take criticism without getting upset.

- **Type of Case: Strategy case based on numbers.**

- **Additional Comments: She asked some great questions in the beginning getting the AOL's subscribers numbers and translating them into percentages and then back again. She started to go off in the wrong direction by trying to define who these new subscribers would be, but she caught herself and looked at the numbers. She also had the instinct to look at the logistics of the offer and the foresight to state that she thought the goal was ambitious. And finally, she rolled with the punches and maintained her sense of humor when the interviewer tested whether she could take criticism.**

+ Disposable Phones

Our client is an entrepreneur who has invented a disposable phone. It's like those phone cards, but instead of just getting the card you get the whole phone. A customer could pay a certain amount for an hours' worth of calls and when that time is up he'd just throw the phone away. Who and how big is the market? What should we charge for an hours' worth of calls? How would we market and distribute the product?

Our client has invented a disposable phone. She wants to know who the target market is, how we'd market and distribute the phones and what we should charge consumers?

Besides the ones mentioned in the question, are there any other objectives that I should be aware of?

– No.

I'd like to know a little bit more about the phone. What is it made of?

– The shell of the phone is constructed of plastic-covered cardboard - sturdier than a milk carton. The buttons are plastic and the insides are electronics. The reception is as good as a regular cellular phone.

Can people receive as well as make calls from these phones? Does each phone have a phone number associated with it?

– Yes. We have purchased the rights to thousands of phones numbers. We can tell when the minutes on a specific phone are used up. The number gets recycled every six months.

There seems to be a number of advantages to this new product. Are there any disadvantages such as health or environmental risks that I should be aware of?

– No.

Because this is a new product, I'd like to price it before I figure out what the market is. I'd like to look at three main ways to price an item; competitive analysis, cost-based pricing and price-based costing.

We need to ask ourselves what is proprietary about our product? Are there similar products out there and what were our R&D costs? Since you said that our client invented this phone I'll assume that we have a patent and that there are no other products like this. Are those fair assumptions?

– Yes. And our R&D costs were modest. One million dollars.

Once the volume is there, what would be our costs per phone?

– The hardware is $1.25 per phone. We are also paying 5 cents per minute.

So using cost-based pricing I'd estimate that it would cost us $1.25 plus 5 cents times 60 minutes equals $1.25 plus $3.00 for the phone connection. We're looking at $4.25 per hour. That doesn't take into account the R&D or marketing costs. Let's assign 75 cents, which brings our costs up to $5.00. If we sell it to the distributors for $7 and have the retailers sell it at $10. Then...

– Before you go on, I want to ask you about why you assigned 75 cents per phone for R&D?

That's a good point; it was an arbitrary assumption. Maybe I should start by looking at the marginal cost of the product, and then I can determine what total fixed costs are associated with the product.

– That's a good plan, but for the purpose of this case, we can stick with your original $5.00.

Okay. Well then next we want to look at what our competitors are selling for. Since there are no direct competitors, we have to look at substitutions like phone cards and cell phones. Phone cards sell for about 8 cents per minute. So an hour would go for $4.80 or $5.00. Which is about half of our cost-based pricing, however they don't provide the phone. The convenience of having the phone is valuable to consumers considering that many pay phones are often broken and you have to dial about a million numbers just to make a local call.

Cell phones, when you figure in the monthly charges work out to about 10 cents per minute, but you have to buy the phone which could run $30 for a cheap phone and you have a minimum monthly fee of $30 a month. So the initial costs are high and our market may not want to lay out that much money. But I'll get to that point when I talk about whom our market is.

Finally, price-based costing. What the market will bear. I'd like to come back to this and do my market sizing based on the $10 per hour.

I'd like to start with our market. Like pre-paid phone cards, our customers are most likely people with little or no credit and who are having a tough time getting a cell phone. Other customers might include international travelers whose cell phone doesn't work in the visiting country. Or even the US traveler who's out of his coverage range. I can also see parents giving a disposable phone to their children for emergency use. And there is always the criminal element that doesn't want to use a phone that can be traced.

I'm assuming that there are 300 million Americans. I'll also assume that there is a fifty percent cell phone penetration. So potentially there are 150 million users. However, I'd estimate that 10 percent of the potential customers would buy these phones, from teenagers on up. So we're looking at around 15 million customers. The extra takes into account middle income parents giving a disposable phone to their children for emergency use and a variety of one-time users like tourists. If we compare this to the cell phone the average person would buy three phones a month, or lay out $30. Which sounds really high to me; 15 million times 3 times a month times 12 months equals 540 million phones.

– Are you serious, 540 million disposable phones per year? Market size it again using a different method.

Okay. I'm going to assume that there are 250 million Americans and that the life expectancy of an American is 75 years. I'm also going to assume that there are even numbers of people in each age category. This means that there are the exact same numbers of 2 year olds as there are 72 year olds. So 250 million divided by 75 equals 3.3 million people per each age category. Let's round it off to 3 million per year.

I'd like to break the age groups down this way, 10 to 20, 21 to 30, 31 to 65 and 66 to 75.

Do you mind if I chart this?

– Be my guest.

% of Age Group	Population	Number of population / users	Total Users	phones / user / month	phones per year
10 – 20	30 million	25%	7.5 million	2	180,000,000
21 – 30	27 million	20%	5.4 million	1	64,800
31 – 65	27 million	10%	2.7 million	.5	16,200
66 – 75	27 million	10%	2.7 million	.5	16,200
Total			18.3 million		295,500,000

My assumptions are that kids under 10 won't be a factor. The group from 10 to 20, basically teenagers, will buy 2 phones per month or 24 phones per year. The age group from 21 to 30, most of them should be able to afford a cell phone, but low income or the unemployed might only be able to afford one a month. The 31 to 65 crowd will already have cell phones so I've lowered expectations. Same with the retired crowd. They may keep one in their car for an emergency.

So if my calculations are correct, I'm estimating that we will sell close to 300 million phones per year. That's quite a bit less than the 540 million we estimated the first time.

– Can you think of factors that would decrease the potential market size?

Sure. I know most cell phone companies offer family plans, so perhaps the number of teenagers who use these phones might be dramatically reduced. I also assume that his would be a habitual purchase, but perhaps someone buys one only when they need them, which would reduce the number of phones used per month. One way to test this assumption might be to see some of the market data on how often consumers buy phone cards, and how long it takes them to use up their minutes. Of course consumers would probably use this phone more often because it's convenient, but it might be a good sanity check.

Back to market sizing. Can we manufacture 300 million phones? Are there that many available phone numbers?

– I'll assume that it will take a while for us to ramp up.

I'm going to jump ahead for a second. We are putting $1.25 into these phones and only using them for an hour. Clearly the construction of these phones can handle more than an hour's use. We should consider marketing them in three to five hour slots. Let's look to see how we are entering this market. Whenever you enter a new market you look at competition, market size, and barriers to entry. We've looked at those already and there aren't any brick walls. So now that we have decided to enter the market we need to figure out how. We can start from scratch, we can acquire an existing player, or we can form a joint venture.

We are too small to acquire anyone. We can start from scratch, which is what I think we've been talking about. However, we need to find a way to get the price per minute down.

– You are losing me. Let's say that you decide to market the phones in three-hour increments. Then what?

You have $1.25 for the hardware and 180 minutes times 5 cents. That totals $9 plus the $1.25. So we're paying $10.25 plus the 75 cents for R&D and marketing. So that's $11 versus the original $15 dollars in costs (3 X the cost of a one-hour phone). In addition, because we'll be making fewer phones we'll save on manufacturing costs, labor costs and shipping costs. So if we almost double it at the retail level consumers will pay $20 for three hours, which is pretty close to the phone cards. Also if we do a joint venture with Sprint or Cingular and use their network then we'd be able to lower the cost per minute to maybe 3 cents per minute. Here, look at these retail prices.

	Phone Card	**Disposable Phone**	**Cell Phone**
One hour	**$5**	**$10**	**$30 monthly fee**
Three hours	**$15**	**$20**	

I rounded off the phone card numbers.

– Okay, that's good. Talk to me about revenues.

If we sell the hour phones to distributors and make $2 per phone, using the 300 million number, we're looking at $600,000,000 in sales, provided that we could produce that many phones. If we produce the 3-hour phone and make $4 per phone, assuming we sell 150 million then we end up generating the same revenues, but as I stated earlier we save on manufacturing, labor and shipping costs.

– What else do you have for me.

Your question also asked me to look at distribution and marketing. I would mirror the phone cards. I would find the phone card distributors and craft a deal with them. The distributor would want in because this new product is going to seriously hurt his phone card business. You could also license the phones and market them with NFL logos and such. Which brings up an interesting point. Do we just want to be in the manufacturing business or do we outsource the manufacturing and focus on the marketing end? Or do we do both?

– What do you think?

I think the decision depends on if and whom she picks as a partner. The client's third option is to license her technology to someone else and just sit back and collect royalties.

– She wants to be involved. Why don't you summarize everything for me?

The client has several options. First, she can just choose to be a manufacturer and sell her phones to a variety of marketing companies and let them compete with each other. Second, she can outsource the manufacturing and concentrate on marketing the phones. Third, she can both manufacture and market the phones.

If she chooses to market the phones I would suggest that she consider $20 for 3 hours. I would distribute them wherever phone cards are sold like convenience stores, record and liquor stores, Kmart, etc. I would license the phones to a number of dealers to put logos on them to bring in extra revenue. She could have really cool designs and colors. We could target urban teenagers and try to make it a fad as well.

I think the market is huge, whether it is 300 million phones is questionable, but it is potentially high. I would want to investigate a joint venture with Sprint or Cingular. They have everything we don't, a network, marketing professionals and capital.

– You did pretty well. I like asking this case. It asks you to think strategically (define the target market). It asks you to structure a problem (p x q = revenue). It tests your math (multiplication is important for case interviews). It tests your ability make assumptions (many people panic and forget that they know; a) how many people are in the USA; and b) what an average cell phone bill is). The fact that you might have been way off and over-estimated the market is not important, in fact it could win you points since consultants need to know how to inflate market sizes to keep clients happy – don't tell anyone I said that.

Type of Case: Strategy / entering a new market / market-sizing

Comments: She asked a number of good, probing questions. The interviewer could follow the logic behind her pricing theory, and she quickly recovered and came up with a second way to size the market. The other thing she did was to question the manufacturing capabilities – will they be able to produce 300 million phones.

+ Disney / Blockbuster

Should Disney buy Blockbuster Video?

Why is Disney considering buying Blockbuster Video?

– Because this is one part of the entertainment market that Disney has little presence in.

Besides making money, is Disney's objective to increase its distribution channels for Disney products?

– Yes. Disney would like to take advantage of those synergies. Customers visit a video store on a regular basis where they might only go to a Disney Store two or three times a year.

Have they thought about just starting up their own chain of video stores?

– They have and they've rejected that strategy. Can you tell me why they might have done that?

Time and real estate. It would take a great deal of time to get everything in place to form an impressive chain of stores. Because the economy has been so good, there aren't many prime retail locations left. Most of the good real estate was snapped up years ago and the turnover is low because the business failure rate is relatively low.

– That's right.

Well, I'd begin by looking at the current video market and then try to forecast where the market is headed. Then if we clear those two barriers, I'd do an analysis of Blockbuster itself.

– Okay.

In the past couple of years, the video rental market has slowed considerably. This has happened for several reasons. First, the economy. Because the economy is doing well people have more disposable income. They don't have to spend their Saturday nights on the couch watching a video. They can afford to go out to dinner, to the movies, or to the ballet. Whatever they want. We would count these as competition for the leisure dollar. Second, even if the economy sours, there are still a number of other types of substitutions out there that are a concern. Things like pay-per-view, Direct TV, and expanded cable.

Internal competition, meaning other video chains, doesn't really concern me. Blockbuster is the biggest and has substantial market share. Everybody rents the same tapes so there is no real product differential, nothing proprietary.

I think the biggest barrier is the future.

– Excuse me?

The rate at which technology is changing troubles me. Soon people will be able to download the movie of their choice off the Internet. There are just too many technological uncertainties. Add that to the fact that there are already a number of substitutes, and the proposition starts to look like a huge risk.

– Would there be any advantages to buying Blockbuster?

There are several advantages. All Disney would have to do is change the sign and redesign the floor to make room for Disney products. They already have the locations, the customer base, the video inventory, the management, and the staff. Another advantage would be cash flow. Video stores generate a lot of cash. A third advantage would be customer flow. People would come in to rent a video and end up buying a Mickey Mouse cereal dish or watch. Disney could make a store visit more of an experience than it would be at any other video chain, and if its prices were competitive it would gain a huge market share. It could easily cross-market in thousands of venues. Ten years ago it was a match made in heaven. Even for the next two, maybe three years. But you need to think long term. I'd concentrate my time and research on the technological changes that are coming and figure out how best to run with those opportunities.

- **Type of case : Entering a new market.**

- **Comments : The candidate was quick to point out that buying Blockbuster is a risky long-term strategy because of all the changes in technology. But she also was able to make a strong argument for the positive side of the acquisition. However, she fell on the side of caution. She might have investigated the option of a joint venture between the two. But overall she did very well.**

Let me put a new twist to this. Our client is now the CEO of Blockbuster. Sales are flat as a pancake and profits have dropped significantly. He has called us in to figure out what's wrong and how to fix it.

So our sole objective is to increase profits?

– That's it.

Has market share remained the same?

– It's slipped a little. Mainly due to increased competition from other video chains like West Coast and Hollywood.

If Blockbuster's market share has remained about the same, then I'll assume that our competitors are having the same types of problems. We already know that sales are slow because of competition, both internal and external. Increased store openings by our competitors is the source of our internal pressure. The external pressures are the substitutions–some technology-driven, like Direct TV and pay-per-view; some economy-driven, like dinner out and the movies.

So on one hand, we need to think of ways to increase sales, and on the other hand, we need to look at how our costs have changed and what we can do about it. If our sales have stayed the same but our profits have dropped, then our costs must have risen.

– Okay.

There are three main ways to increase sales: increase prices, get more customers in the door, and get those customers to spend more once we have them in the store. How are our prices?

– Our prices are exactly the same as our competitors.

Okay, so that eliminates a price hike. I'm assuming that our traffic has dropped off a little or remained about the same. So we need to come up with a marketing campaign that will give more people a reason to come into the store. And third, once they're in the store, we need to get them to rent more videos, or spend money on impulse items like magazines or popcorn.

– What else?

I'd like to analyze our revenue streams. I'll assume that we get revenues from video rentals, video sales, video game rentals, and miscellaneous items. Can you tell me how those streams break down in percentages of sales?

– Video rentals are broken into two categories–new releases, which are videos that are two years old or less, and classics, which are more than two years old. New releases make up 60% of revenues, classics make up 10%. Video sales, both new and previously viewed, make up 20%, and video game rentals make up 5%. Miscellaneous sales are another 5%.

Wow. New releases make up 60%. I guess the number that throws me the most is the classics at 10%. First, those tapes are already paid for so the rental income on them pretty much goes straight to the bottom line. So if we can figure out a way to increase their rentals that would be a big plus. The second thing about that number is, why is so much space devoted to such a small component of the revenues? Think about it. When you walk into a Blockbuster all the new releases are on the outside walls. All the classics take up that huge space in the middle. Maybe we should think about how to better utilize that space. Maybe all the classic videos can be stacked in the back and we have a half a dozen computers throughout the store with 30-second classic movie trailers.

Customers could choose by genre or star and a list of movies would pop up and then they could view the trailer. The computer could also tell you whether the movie was in stock. Because as they are situated now, I feel it's wasted space.

– Interesting. What about costs?

I mentioned earlier that if sales are flat and profits are down, then costs must have shot up. I see the major costs as cost of goods sold–the cost of buying the tapes, labor costs, rent, and marketing. I imagine marketing costs have inched up, and they should. Even though

Blockbuster has great brand recognition, we still need to remind people that renting a video can be a great time. I'll assume that rent has inched up as well. Because the economy is doing well, retail space is at a premium and landlords can increase rents. I think that the major increase has been labor costs. Again, because of the economy and low unemployment, workers are hard to find. Two years ago you were probably paying minimum wage, now you have to pay $8 an hour just to compete with the McDonald's down the street. One strategy to boost profits might be to pray for a recession. This economy is killing us.

– (Laughs) Probably not my first choice.

The last major cost is cost of inventory. When I was in high school we sold Christmas trees and wreaths to raise money for the sailing team. The first year we bought the trees through a distributor and made $6 a tree. The second year, we took a road trip up to New Hampshire and bought directly from the grower, contracted someone to deliver the trees, and made $20 a tree. Why can't Blockbuster go directly to the studios for the major blockbusters?

– How do you see that working? Do you think we can just cut out the distributor?

On certain films, yes. Blockbuster is one of their biggest customers. You think they're going to cut us off? This is how I envision it. Okay, say *The Lord of the Rings* was coming to video soon. Blockbuster goes to New Line and says we were thinking of buying one million copies of *The Lord of the Rings* through the distributor at, let's say, $12 a copy. But we will buy two million copies if we can buy it directly from you for $8. Saving us $4 a copy. In addition, we will give you 5% of all the rental income on those tapes for the first 60 days, if you float us the tapes for 60 days.

– Go on.

Well, first, we have twice the number of copies of the video in our store. So everyone who wants to see *The Lord of the Rings* can pretty much get a copy the next time they visit Blockbuster. So there is one reason for people to come to Blockbuster. But this is the really cool part. Let's look at it on a per store basis. Say each store gets 200 copies.

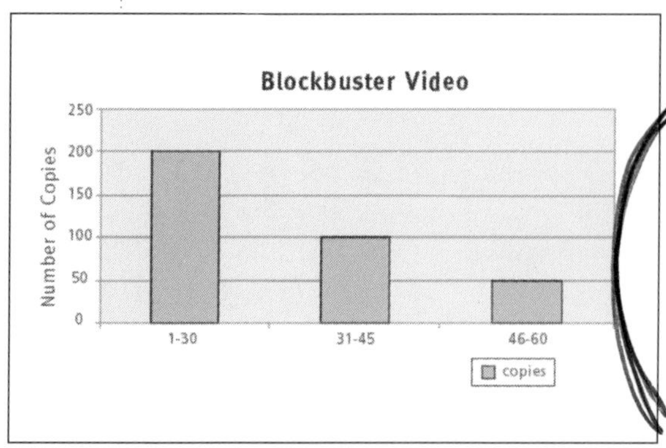

Can I draw a diagram?

– Be my guest.

For the first 30 days we have 200 copies available. And assume that those 200 copies are rented 90% of the time. So that's 200 x 30 x .90 = 5,400 @ $3.50 = $18,900 or $19,000.

For the next 15 days (days 31–45) we have 100 copies on the shelf. And assume that those copies get rented 75% of the time. So that's 100 X 15 X .75 = 1,125 @ $3.50 = $3,937.50 or $4,000. But we also have 100 videos that we can now sell as previously viewed @ $10 each. So add another $1,000. So that's $5,000. And remember we only paid $8 each so not only did we collect the rental income, but we're selling them for more than we paid.

For the final 15 days (days 46–60) we have 50 copies available. Assume that those copies are rented 50% of the time. So that's 50 x 15 x .50 = 375 @ $3.50 = $1,312.50 or $1,300. But we also have another 100 videos that we can now sell at $7.99 each. So add another $800. So that's $2,100.

Okay. We brought in $19,000 plus $5,000 plus $2,100 which equals $26,100 in revenues, minus the 5% that goes back to the studio which is $1,305 or $1,300. So this store has brought in about $25,000 even before they've had to pay a dime for the videos. And when we do have to pay for them we only have to pay $1,600.

– We have about two minutes left. Can you summarize?

Sure. First to increase revenues I'd invest in a large marketing campaign focusing on the fact that we have more copies of recent releases than anyone else. Second, I'd stack the classics in the back and install interactive computer monitors, and then make better use of the space in the middle of the store. Maybe bring in some high profit items or something that would attract more people to the store. Third, I'd bypass the distributors and go cut an exclusive deal with the studios. And finally, I'd set up a group that will review all the new technologies out there and try to figure out a way for Blockbuster to compete through renting movies via the Internet.

– Very good. There's someone else I'd like you to meet.

◗ Type of case : Increasing the bottom line.

◗ Comments : This was an incredible answer. Not only did she analyze the problem using the classic Profits = (Revenues – Costs) x Volume, she came up with an extraordinary plan to increase profits and cash flow. And she graphed it! She started with the revenue side first, identifying the revenue streams and picking out and focusing on a number that struck her as odd (classics revenues are only 10%). She was also quick to focus on the skyrocketing labor costs.

+ The Gap

You are the marketing vice president of The Gap and things couldn't be better. In 1998, Gap Inc. (U.S.) spent around 4.4% of its total sales—approximately $400 million—on advertising expenses; in the fourth quarter of 1998, the company posted a 45.6% rise in earnings.

However, your director of research has just come in and unloaded a bomb. Despite the great sales at The Gap and Baby Gap, "Generation Y" isn't buying into your products. This is a significant problem because Generation Y represents a buying force of 60 million compared to Gen-Xers at 17 million. The Baby Boomers, who are your best customers, will be slowly diminishing over the next 10 years.

Your challenge is to figure out how to reach Generation Y. How do you secure the future of your company?

So the real question here is, how do we tap into the Generation Y mindset and market to ensure future growth of Gap products? I assume that's the main objective as well.

– That's exactly right.

I'm assuming that the majority of The Gap's customers are Baby Boomers and Gen-Xers.

– Correct.

Gen–Yers are how old?

– Gen-Yers are 4 to 19.

What else can you tell me about the Gen-Yers?

– I'd rather have you make some assumptions.

We can go a couple of ways on this. The marketers that capture Gen Y's attention do so by bringing their message to the place these kids congregate, whether it's the Internet, cable television, or a snowboarding or skateboarding tournament. They think like kids, they've researched them, they've lived among them.

This is really an interesting question. We need to look at strategies for entering a new market and developing new products, as well as competitive response strategies.

The first step is research. Who are our major competitors and why? How big are they and what has their marketing strategy been? What kind of market share do they have? Are they a fad, or will they be around for a while? In addition, we need to research the Gen-Yers. We could send out teams of young college or high school researchers and have them gather market research through primary and secondary sources.

– So we do our research. What else?

To enter a new market we can start from scratch, acquire an existing player, or enter a joint venture. Starting from scratch means starting a new division directed at Gen-Yers, but keeping our association with The Gap a secret. Acquiring an existing player would just be a matter of money and opportunity. We could allow them to keep their independence, but they could furnish us with product ideas and marketing strategies. Or we could form a strategic alliance with an already hip product and hope for a positive association. One example might be Dawson's Creek on The WB.

Developing a new product would have to be under the new company. I don't care how innovative the product is, it would be a tough sell under the Gap label. It's the same sort of problem Oldsmobile had with the Gen-Xers. And the tag line, "The Gap: Not your father's pants" does nothing for me. So we'd market under a new name. Which is fine. Look at Disney, they have several different studios that produce movies for different audiences.

The third strategy was the competitive response. How do we react if a competitor introduces a new product or picks up market share? There are five main ways. Acquire a competitor, merge with a competitor, copy a competitor, hire the competitor's top management, and increase our profile with a marketing campaign.

There are some commonalities among those strategies. The chief one is to acquire one of our competitors. If they refuse to be bought, we'll lure their top management away, start a new division, and give them their freedom in running it.

– Anything else?

One last thing. I'd re-evaluate our Internet presence, maybe place more ads in strategic Generation Y sites to see what the response is.

- Type of case : Entering a new market, developing a new product, and competitive response.

- Comments : Not only did the candidate come up with some great suggestions to research the Gen-Yers, she was quick to figure out that this question covered three scenarios. She logically addressed each scenario using the appropriate outlines, then conducted a cost-benefit analysis, weighing the advantages and disadvantages of each option.

The Growth Strategies Case Scenario would have been applicable here as well.

+ Micky D's

Our client is McDonalds. Their main markets have been young men and children. In the last three years they have seen a deterioration in some of their kids' business. Sales of Happy Meals have fallen around 6 percent a year, three years in a row. The Happy Meal, which consists of an entrée (hamburger, cheeseburger or chicken nuggets), small fries, small drink and a free toy accounts for more than 20 percent of US transactions, or approximately $3.5 billion in annual revenues (according to the WSJ 1/31/03). The Happy Meal also generates sales from the accompanying adult.

McDonalds has dominated the kids' fast food market since 1976 but has been losing market share to competitors like Wendy's, Burger King and Yum Brands Inc, which owns Taco Bell, Pizza Hut and KFC.

McDonalds wants to know what it can do to turn this trend around and become profitable again. McDonalds posted a loss for the first time in its history in Q4 2002.

Let's make sure I understand the question. McDonalds has been losing market share in the kids' market for the last three years. Happy Meals sales have fallen off about 6 percent a year for the last three years. A six percent loss represents around a $175 million decline last year alone. Competitors like Wendy's, Burger King and the Yum restaurants have been stealing away market share and McDonalds wants to know what it can do about it. Are there any other objectives that we should be aware of?

– They want to know how they can become profitable again.

Has the overall market for kids' meals declined?

– No. In fact it has risen a bit, about 3 percent.

Who drives the decision on where to eat? Is it the kids or the adult?

– Good question. Most of the time it's the kid's decision.

I'd venture that most kids are more interested in the free toy than whether they're eating a McDonalds burger or one from BK. Have they noticed whether a particular toy drives sales?

– Yes. In the late 1990's sales hit an all-time high when McDonald's were giving out teenie beanie babies.

Has the popularity and quality of the toys declined?

– Some might say yes.

I'd like to compare the toys that BK is giving out to the ones McDonalds have been giving out over the past three years. Are there restrictions; cost, size or type of toys that can be handed out?

– Yes. McDonald's signed a ten-year agreement with Disney that prohibits them to hand out toys from their competitors. In 2001 and 2002 about half the toys given away were Disney related.

I read in the Wall Street Journal that Disney is losing money as well. Part of the reason is that they've had some flops at the box office. I'll assume that McDonalds was required to use these flop-related toys in their Happy Meals while BK can do promotions with The Simpsons, Rugrats and SpongeBob SquarePants. So if the decision of where to eat is made by the child and he sees an ad with a SpongeBob SquarePants toy at Burger King that's where he's going. How many years left in the Disney contract?

– Five.

I'd see if we could renegotiate the Disney contract without irking them. This would allow us some flexibility with their competitors. All it takes is one big Disney hit to get a nice bump in sales. Maybe we can sell Disney DVDs or other merchandise at our stores, or maybe go back to the Disney classics for toys like Mickey Mouse. Disney owns the ABC Network, and since the trend seems to be towards television characters, maybe pull some characters from ABC's Saturday morning cartoon line-up.

– Okay. What else?

Is there a price difference between the Happy Meal at McDonalds and the price of the kids' meal at say Burger King?

– Yes. McDonalds prices have been creeping higher.

I'll assume that part of the increase is the cost of the toy.

– That's a fair assumption.

So right now we know that Burger King has more popular toys and lower prices. I'll assume that lowering the prices in not an option, but we can still run special promotions for the adult meals. We can investigate the strategy of getting more kids coming in together. Bring a friend to McDonalds and the adults eat for $2. It's the reverse marketing of kids eat for free.

– Interesting. There is still a big component to this case that you are missing.

I was just getting around to that. You said the two main markets were teenage boys and kids. McDonalds might want to think about focusing on the adult that brings the children in.

– You just said that adults eat for $2.

No, this is different. How about a gift for mom with the purchase of a meal bought with a Happy Meal? It could be a simple gift like lip-gloss. We could also investigate a rewards program that so many other retailers have. Spend $25 on Happy Meals and receive a $10 off coupon for a facial at Elizabeth Grady's or buy ten Happy Meals and get your next one free. One thing we haven't talked about is customer loyalty.

I think we are seeing a decline in customer loyalty in the fast food business. The decision on where to eat lunch may have more to do with location, menu specials and product choice. Are fast food hamburgers really that different? Or is it like a Coke and Pepsi relationship. You may have a favorite, but one is easily substituted for the other.

– Okay, but you're still missing a big component to this case.

Big is the key word here. I've been hearing a lot about child obesity lately. How today's kids are less active and heavier than they were just a generation ago. So what about putting new items on the Happy Meal menu. Things that are healthy like carrot sticks, peanut butter and jelly sandwiches, maybe apple slices.

– Good, that's one of the things I was looking for. Anything else?

Yes. We may want to have a secondary draw - another reason for kids to come to McDonalds. We might think about having a video game arcade. It would be another revenue stream and give them a reason to hangout and spend more money.

– Okay. Why don't you take a minute to summarize for me?

Because kids drive the decision on where to eat, and because they care more for the toy than the meal, McDonald's has to focus on delivering more popular toys. I think that they should try to renegotiate their contract with Disney in order to give themselves more flexibility in picking cool and popular toys. I'd also focus on the moms, with a two-prong approach. First, I'd offer mom a gift as well and second, I'd offer healthy meals. This is important because if the decision is a toss up mom is going to choose the restaurant that offers her child a healthier fare. I'd start a customer loyalty program where moms could redeem points toward McDonalds' food, Disney merchandise or Elizabeth Grady facials. And finally, I put in video or arcade games, something that will draw in the teenage crowd.

– Good answer.

Type of case: Strategy, competitive response, increasing sales.

Comments: The student asked good questions and took the information given and hit on all the major points. It may have seemed like he was getting into too much detail, but in this case it was appropriate to come up with a few ideas as well as a broad strategy.

+ City of Portland, Maine

Twenty years ago, Portland floated a bond to build a 1,000-foot dock. The dock was leased by The Bath Irons Works, a division of General Dynamics, to repair Navy ships. Bath Iron Works recently announced that it is leaving Portland to consolidate its operations in Virginia. City officials underestimated the amount of time needed to pay off the bond, and now Portland will have to eat the rest of the debt.

Portland officials have decided that they need to do something to cover the debt payments. They have decided to ask the state to fund a $15.6 million plan to renovate the dock and terminal with the goal of attracting large cruise ships to the port.

You are the chairperson of the State Appropriations Committee. What do you need to know to make the decision to fund the project? While we understand that politics will play a key role in the decision, please look at this as a business decision and not a political one.

I'm the chairperson of the State Appropriations Committee. I need to make a business decision on whether or not the state should allocate $15.6 million for the dock renovation project.

– That's correct.

I take it that the objectives are threefold. First, to pay off the outstanding debt. Second, to revitalize the dock so it doesn't become an eyesore. And third, to bring additional tourist dollars into Portland and tax revenues to the state.

– You forgot one. To bring jobs to the area so that many of the workers can be rehired and so the state doesn't have to shell out unemployment and other benefits.

Do any cruise ships come to Portland now?

– Yes. Cruise ships have been coming to Portland for a number of years. In 1995 we had 15 ships, in 1996 we had 25 ships, in 1997 we had 26 ships, in 1998 we had 17 ships, and in 1999 we are forecasting 16 ships.

Why the decline in recent years?

– Two reasons. First, the current facility is awful. Passengers have to walk a half-mile through an industrial site just to reach the waterfront tourist shops. The walk is long, dirty, and noisy. Second, ships started visiting other ports, like Boston, Bar Harbor, and Nova Scotia, which have newer and better facilities.

Is there any indication that if we renovate the dock, the ships will come?

– In the cruise industry, demand follows supply. Cruise lines are expanding and they need new places to go. Okay, I feel as if you're trying to get me to answer the question for you. What would you need to do in order to make a decision?

Well, I would do a couple of things. I'd conduct my due diligence, learning as much about the dock and operation as possible. I'd go up and investigate the site and have a first-hand look at the situation. Would the new dock be closer to the waterfront shops than the current dock? Maybe we should be renovating the current dock. Next, I'd contact the various cruise lines like Carnival and Royal Caribbean to see if this is something that would attract them to Portland. And if so, how often they would visit and what the city can do to make itself more attractive as a port.

I'd do a quantitative analysis on how many passengers would have to come through and how much they would have to spend in Portland to make this feasible. I'd investigate whether the waterfront area can handle an influx of 2,000 people all at one time. And I'd see how committed the city was. How much is the city putting up? We really have three choices here. Make the investment as requested. Pay off the remaining $3 million dollar outstanding debt. Or do nothing. The last thing I'd do is figure out the effects it would have on the state if we did nothing. If this area loses the shipyard and nothing comes to take its place, we'll lose not only the shipyard, but also the waterfront area. There will be no one around to support the shops and restaurants. So property values go down, tax revenues go down, you have more people on unemployment, and eventually the state may have to bail out the city on other financial matters as well.

– Better. I know we touched on this, but what would some of the benefits and revenue streams be that the state would get in return?

First, we'd create jobs. Construction jobs as well as service jobs. This would bring in new taxes, as well as keep some people off welfare. Second, we'd receive taxes from the tourist dollars and from the increased revenues from the waterfront shops. Third, I think Portland citizens would come down to the waterfront area and spend their money as well.

- **Type of case : Turnaround (strategy).**
- **Comments : Good strong analysis. Nothing fancy here. She asked all the important questions to gather relevant data. However, she did get into a little trouble by asking too many open-ended questions and making the interviewer feel as if he were answering the question for her.**

+ Entertainment Spin-off

A large diversified company ($25 billion in sales) has a $10 billion entertainment division (not unlike Disney or Paramount) that has movies, theme parks, and music.

The chair is thinking of breaking up the entertainment group into two separate companies. They would be spun-off and the parent company would maintain a majority position in both. Each company would conduct an IPO (initial public offering), selling 17% of its shares on the stock market. This would raise a large amount of new capital to fund expansion.

The chair is unsure how to group the divisions. Does he put film and theme parks together, film and music together, or theme parks and music together?

How should the chair group the companies, and what is the downside to pulling this off?

To quickly review, a large corporation wants to spin off its entertainment division into two separate companies and then take them public. The chair wants us to determine which units in this division belong together and what problems the company will face pulling this off.

– That's right.

The objective is to raise new capital to fund expansion for these units. Anything else?

– That's all you need to be concerned with.

What other businesses does the corporation run?

– Non-entertainment, and not relevant to the question.

It would seem to me that it makes the most sense to keep the film and theme parks together. Many of the theme park attractions are based on major films, like *Jaws*, *Indiana Jones*, and *Star Wars*. It just seems as if there are more synergies between those two than either one has with music.

– What else?

Let's talk risk. A record company signs a hundred new artists each year. They pay only for the cost of producing the CD, which is just a couple of thousand dollars. Marketing costs are much less than film, and now with so much music being marketed on the Internet, the costs are even lower. Out of that hundred, maybe two or three will hit it big, half will muddle along, and the rest will go nowhere. So the investment is small and the payoff could be big.

In film, a studio may release 15 films and hope for one big hit. But the investment is huge. The average cost of a studio film is around $40 million. Add onto that marketing costs and you're looking at $65 million per film.

– So what are you saying?

I'm saying that the movie studios need the tie-in to the theme parks for their cash flow and stability. However, I do want to state that if the economy sours, the theme parks and film division will suffer the most. If these divisions are going to leave the nest, then some of that newly raised capital should be set aside.

– Do you think the economy is going to sour?

The point is, you never know. If it's open for discussion, I'd like to visit the idea of spinning these divisions off. It seems there might be ways to raise the capital for these divisions other than going public–say a bond offering or issuing more stock from the parent.

– That's interesting. Can you summarize the advantages and disadvantages of spinning off?

The advantage of going public is raising the extra capital. For the management of those divisions, the advantage is being able to run your own show. The disadvantage is that you lose the protection of a big corporation.

– Thank you. Next.

Type of case : Spin-off. Spin-off?! That's not on my list! Yes, sometimes you're going to get a question that doesn't fit neatly into our 10 case scenarios. If you encounter such a case, ask clarifying questions and use experience and common sense to guide your answer.

Comments : She did okay. As she should have, she asked a lot of good questions and raised some valid points. The interviewer was sort of a jerk, which makes it hard. Part of the excitement or challenge of interviewing is that you never know who is going to interview you or what kind of mood he'll be in.

+ Digital Hollywood

Our client is the president of a major Hollywood movie studio. She has called us in to help her decide whether the studio should switch to digital production and distribution. What are the pluses and minuses of such a decision, and what hurdles will she face?

We are working with the president of a major Hollywood studio who needs to decide whether her studio should switch over to digital production and distribution. We need to help her make a good decision by analyzing the advantages and disadvantages of this move.

– Right.

What are our objectives? Cost savings? To be an industry leader?

– Cost savings is the main one.

Can you explain what digital production/distribution mean? I'm unfamiliar with the terms.

– Many movies are shot on film, then edited digitally, and converted back to film. They are then distributed in the film format to theaters.

Is the quality of digital better or worse than film?

– Recently, the quality of digital has finally equaled that of film.

What are the other studios thinking?

– We'll meet with the other major studios next week, but we want to come up with our own independent decision before that meeting.

I'm going to make some assumptions. The first assumption is that it has to be cheaper to reproduce a movie on a CD than on film. I think I read that one copy of a movie on film costs around $2,000 while a CD can be copied for about $2. And if you're talking about a thousand theaters, that's a substantial savings. Two million versus two thousand. The second assumption I'm making has to do with distribution. A physical film needs to be shipped by courier, where a digital film could be received by the theater owners by satellite or email or cable. Again, that's another cost savings. Figure a thousand theaters at $50 each, that's $50,000. Also, delivery can be made in a matter of minutes instead of hours or days. The third assumption is that electronic delivery of feature films to theaters could eliminate the middleman, the distributor, which would save millions.

The fourth assumption has to do with storage. Once on CD, the copy will always be pristine. You don't have to keep it stored in a climate-controlled storage area, and it takes up less space.

– So far so good. What else?

On the negative side, if we increase the distribution system and create almost a pay-per-view system for theaters, our middle-of-the-road movies and stinkers will get yanked from the theaters much more quickly.

– Makes sense. Go on.

The other concern is whether the theaters are ready for the switch. I would imagine there would be new technology to acquire, and I'll assume it's expensive.

– You're right. The new technology would probably run $90,000 per theater. If you run a 10-screen megaplex, that's $900,000 in capital outlay.

There will probably be opportunities to rent the equipment. And what about the small theaters? I imagine a period where studios would have to release the movie on both film and CD. There also have to be other costs for the theater owners, like data storage hardware, satellite dishes, etc. I think it will be a slow conversion. But my biggest fear is piracy. Is the encryption technology there? What if a master is stolen, either from a theater or picked off from a satellite? High-quality cheap copies could be manufactured and sold quickly and the studio would lose millions.

– You've brought up some good points. So what do you recommend?

My suggestion would be to meet with the other studios. This is really an industry decision, not an individual studio decision. I would also want to meet with the theater owners and find out how we can help them convert over to digital, because it's in both our best interests to do so. Anything we can do to expedite the process should be carefully considered.

– What if I told you that as a major studio, we are also a major distributor?

I would expand my research to include a cost-benefit analysis to make sure the gains outweigh the losses. But in the end, I still believe that it's an industry decision.

– Thanks.

- **Type of case : Reducing costs.**

- **Comments : This wasn't a typical "reduce the costs" question. It was really more of a strategy question than an operations question. The interviewee drew information about CDs from what he knew about music CDs and DVD discs and built on that. He wasn't afraid to ask about what he didn't know, e.g., "What are digital production and distribution?" One thing he didn't know is that this major studio is also a major distributor and he should have done a cost-benefit analysis to find out if the client would be saving more than it would be losing.**

Lastly, the candidate was wise enough to realize that in the end, this is an industry decision, not an individual studio decision.

+ The Ford SUV Stops Climbing

The Ford Motor Company has watched the sales of its SUVs decline. What do you think the problems are and what can Ford do about it?

Ford has been losing sales of its SUVs. They want to know why and what can be done about it.

– That's right.

Besides identifying and fixing the problem are there any other objectives I should be aware of?

– Profits. We're always concerned about profits.

How many SUVs does Ford produce and which ones are getting hit the hardest?

– Ford produces thirteen SUVs under five major brands, Ford, Mercury, Lincoln, Mazda, and Land Rover. The two that they are most concerned about are the Ford Explorer down 22.6 percent and the Ford Excursion down 36 percent.

How are the sales of the other SUVs?

– Let's call them flat.

How are Ford's overall sales?

– Down 11 percent.

Have Ford's competitors had the same problem? In other words, is this an industry-wide problem or one that is just confined to Ford? How about the overall auto industry?

– Good question. The overall auto industry is down. Toyota sales are down 11 percent and the Camry, which has been the best selling car in the US over the last several years, has dropped by 45 percent. While the other companies have seen the sales of their SUVs slow down, they haven't taken the hit that Ford has taken.

So it's an industry problem?

– Are you asking me or telling me?

Sounds like an overall industry problem to some degree. I'm going to make some assumptions. Certainly, the Firestone tire crisis has taken its toll on the Explorer sales.

– Yes, you can assume that 7 percent, almost a third of the decline was due to the Firestone crisis as you call it. But that doesn't explain the even bigger slump by the Ford Excursion.

Then let's look at gas prices, they've topped $2 a gallon in some states.

– As they did last year. Ford had its biggest year last year. Most consumers weren't deterred by high gas prices. And high gas prices would have hit other SUVs as well, particularly the Ford Expedition which has the gas mileage of a tank.

Increased competition, both internally from within Mother Ford and from external competitors. It's possible that by producing so many SUVs Ford is cannibalizing its own market.

– Okay I'll buy that, but what does Ford do about it?

Maybe it doesn't do anything about it. We need to figure out if these consumers are trading up or not. If they are trading up, then that's a good thing. If not, the Explorer has to come up with additional incentives to win customers back.

– What else?

Since the overall SUV market has declined, I'll assume that a small part of that is due to environmental concerns.

– Maybe. Is that it?

No. Every time you read the newspaper you see an article about people getting laid off. Consumer confidence is down, the stock market is down and some folks are taking a bunker mentality. They've curtailed spending, particularly on high-cost items like cars.

– What if Ford offered generous loan programs?

As they did last year. With interest rates at a thirty-year low I think people who were going to buy a car might have done so last year. You mentioned that Ford had its best year last year, which means that the percentage drops are coming from a new high. Maybe the sales numbers aren't that bad, it's just that last year's numbers were that good.

– Good point. So recap for me why this is happening then tell me what you would do.

Ford's SUV sales have slumped for several reasons. I'd like to categorize them into internal and external factors. First, the Firestone crisis did a number on the Explorer's reputation, and it might take several years to recover. Second, Ford produces thirteen different SUVs under five brands. There is a good chance that they are cannibalizing their own market share. Now that can be either a good thing or a bad thing depending on whether the customers are trading up or trading down. Third, I'd go back and evaluate the numbers over the past five years. Last year was a banner year for Ford, so they we are dropping from the peak. This might be a signal that the SUV market is on the decline for several external reasons as well.

The first external reason would be the economy. Consumer confidence is low and unemployment is growing so people are saving money. And because the economy is souring, small things like high gas prices and low mileage start to add up in the consumer's mind. The second external factor is increased competition from other auto companies, which not only brings out new SUVs but other cars that consumers view as a substitution.

– So what would you tell Ford to do?

Before I answer that, I'd like to make one more assumption and that is 2001 inventories remain high. Is that a fair assumption?

– Yes.

Then I'd do four things. I want to decrease my inventory so I'd increase my marketing and tie in a PR campaign to combat the bad press from the Firestone crisis. I'd tie an attractive incentive program maybe .09 percent financing. I'd evaluate the overall SUV market to determine whether so much emphasis should continue to be directed toward the SUV market. If the answer to that is yes, I'd consider marketing a SUV lite.

– A SUV lite? What's that?

Most people purchase a SUV because they like sitting up high, they like the powerful engine as well as the generous room inside an Explorer. I would venture to guess that most SUV drivers have never gone off-road. So if you make a SUV Lite by taking away the 4-wheel drive which they hardly ever use you're left with a lighter SUV, one that would get better gas mileage, it would drive more smoothly and more quietly because you wouldn't have to use the off-road tires. The driver would still sit up high and they would still have plenty of room.

– That's an interesting thought. You did a good job.

- **Type of Case: Strategy / increasing sales**

- **Comments: The student did a good job of analyzing why sales have slumped, particularly picking up on the fact that with 13 SUVs Ford is most likely cannibalizing its own sales.**

+ Case Index

Business Cases – – – – – Type

1. **Case of Bud** – – – – – Strategy
2. **Rock and Roll Suicide** – – – – – Pricing
3. **House of Pizza** – – – – – Entering a new market and acquisition
4. **Eastern Training Network** – – – – – Competitive Response
5. **Starbucks** – – – – – Increase sales and growth
6. **Snow Job** – – – – – Strategy based on numbers
7. **Pop Corn City** – – – – – Starting a new business
8. **Cow Brothers Premium Ice Cream** – – – – – Increase sales and growth
9. **Jamaican Battery Enterprise** – – – – – Strategy, entering a new market, and market sizing
10. **Coke** – – – – – Strategy based on numbers
11. **World Spacelines** – – – – – Strategy, entering a new market, and market sizing
12. **Savannah Jane's Laundromat** – – – – – Acquisition and turnaround
13. **Hair raising** – – – – – Market-sizing and pricing
14. **Pay Phones** – – – – – Increase sales and growth
15. **Brazilian Soda Manufacturer** – – – – – Market-sizing and pricing
16. **Yellow Stuff Chemical Company** – – – – – Entering a new market
17. **College Mail** – – – – – Strategy and marketing
18. **Road to Ruin** – – – – – Market-sizing, new product and pricing
19. **The Gas Company** – – – – – Reducing Costs
20. **Texas Star Markets** – – – – – Entering a new market
21. **Longest-lasting Light Bulb** – – – – – Pricing
22. **eTailers** – – – – – Increasing sales
23. **Screw Tops for Fine Wine** – – – – – Strategy and marketing
24. **Fuel Efficiency** – – – – – Pricing
25. **New York Opera** – – – – – Growth Strategies
26. **High Speed Train** – – – – – Entering a new market
27. **Bull Moose Financial** – – – – – Reducing Costs
28. **Getting into Diapers** – – – – – Market-sizing, entering a new market
29. **eOfficemanager** – – – – – Starting a new business
30. **WIVY FM Radio** – – – – – Increasing the Bottom Line

- **Archive Cases ––––– Type**

1. **AOL** ––––– Strategy case based on numbers
2. **Disposable Phones** ––––– Strategy, entering a new market, and market sizing
3. **Disney/Blockbuster** ––––– Entering a new market and increasing the bottom line
4. **The Gap** ––––– Entering a new market, developing a new product, and competitive response
5. **Mickey D's** ––––– Strategy, competitive response, and increasing sales
6. **City of Portland** ––––– Turnaround
7. **Entertainment Spin** ––––– Spin–off
8. **Digital Hollywood** ––––– Reducing costs
9. **A Ford SUV Stops Climbing** ––––– Strategy and increasing sales

+ Case Questions Without Answers

Below are case questions that were given by top-tier consulting firms. I've broken them down by first, second and third rounds. For an up-to-date list go to CaseQuestions.com and click on Recent Cases.

First Round

- How many airplanes are in United States airspace at 10:00 on a weekday morning?
- Hindustan Motors of Madras, India has been bleeding for the past 18 months, losing a lot of money and experiencing declining sales. Why is this happening and how do we fix it?
- A man who owns an oil and gas platform is offering to sell it. Would you buy it?

Second Round

- The Tube, the London underground, is a mess. It's too crowded, too expensive, and constantly breaking down. The government is fighting over how to fix and fund it. The train drivers' union says it will go on strike unless the government guarantees that there will be no layoffs. What steps would you take to "fix" the problem?
- How would you increase recruitment and retention in the military?
- The U.S. Post Office lost millions last year. How would you advise the new CEO to turn the Post Office around.
- Your client is a large food manufacturer that has had pressure from shareholders to increase revenues. The manufacturer has had slow growth in North America and Europe with top-line growth of 2%. Your client has heard that the developing markets can be profitable, and wants to know if it should invest.

Third Round

- A mobile phone manufacturer is trying to decide whether it should reduce prices to gain market share. What do you tell him?
- A company developed a prototype of what it hopes to be an innovative medical product. Designed to address serious injuries, the product is a malleable material that can act as a synthetic bone, eliminating the need to fuse a severely fractured bone back together with a cumbersome and painful process of rods and pins. The company is in the early stages and would like to know what some of the issues might be around this product. What are some of the things you'd like to know before proceeding with this venture?
- A computer manufacturer such as IBM has developed a new computer that is 100 times more powerful than existing models. What should be their marketing strategy and how should they price it?

- Last year, lawsuits cost corporations $200 billion compared with $70 billion in 1990. How would you advise a roundtable of CEOs to promote tort reform.
- A major manufacturer of premium large appliances has been losing market share over the past two years. They want to find out why, and what they can do about it.
- Company Q manufactures wheelchairs. They've designed the ultimate wheelchair that can climb stairs and can raise its seat to 6 feet in the air so the occupant can reach upper shelves. A regular wheelchair costs x, a motorized wheelchair costs 2x, and this ultimate wheelchair costs 4x. Who is the market? What is the market size? And should company Q proceed with the rollout of the ultimate wheel chair?
- How does American Express make its money from travelers checks?

If you have been begged, bribed, or blackmailed into helping your friend(s) prepare for case questions, here are some hints.

Your prep

- Read the question and answer all the way through before giving the case.
- Be aware that there are multiple "right" answers.
- It's all right to give them help if they lose their way.
- Don't cop a know-it-all attitude.

Things to watch for at the beginning

- Are they writing down the case information?
- Is there a long silence between the end of the question and the beginning of their answer?
- Are they summarizing the question?
- Are they asking about the client's objective(s)?
- Are they asking clarifying questions about the company, the industry, the competition, and the product?
- Are they laying out a logical structure for their answer?

Things to watch and listen for during the course of the question

- Are they enthusiastic and do they project a positive attitude?
- Listen for the logic of their answer. Is it making good business sense?
- Is their answer well-organized?
- Are they stating their assumptions clearly?
- Are they being creative?
- Are they engaging, bringing you into the question and turning the case into a conversation?
- Are they asking probing questions?
- Are they quantifying their answer?
- Are they asking for help or guidance?

Review list

- Was their answer well-organized? Did they manage their time well?
- Did they get bogged down in details?
- Did they seem to go off on a tangent?
- Did they ask probing questions?
- Did they use business terms and buzzwords correctly?
- Did they have trouble with math, multiplying, and percentage calculation?
- Did they try to get you to answer the question for them?
- Were they coachable? Did they pick up on your hints?
- Did they speak without thinking?
- Did they have a positive attitude?
- Did they summarize their answer?

Final analysis

- Did they take your criticism well?
- Did they defend themselves without sounding defensive?

Aftermath

- Go out on the town.

9 : Final Analysis

In the end it's only you against the beast (the case question, not the interviewer). We can't be there with you, but we've given you the tools to feel confident and to have a good time. If you're excited about the challenge and the interview, then you're headed into the right profession. If you dread what's coming, you may want to re-evaluate your career choice. When discussing career choices, Winston Churchill advised his children, "Do what you like, but like what you do." It's all about having fun.

It's easy to forget that the firms know you can do the work–they wouldn't be interviewing you if they didn't think you were smart enough to succeed. Now it's just time to prove them right.

Back-of-the-envelope question : A type of case question, most often a market-sizing question, that asks you to make an educated estimate of something. The back-of-the-envelope question received its name because the questions used to start with, "You're on an airplane, with no books, phone, or any resources. On the back of an envelope figure…." An example: "How many pairs of boxers are sold in the U.S. each year?"

Barrier to entry : Factor (such as capital requirements, access to distribution channels, proprietary product technology, or government policy) that would inhibit a company when entering a new market.

Benchmark : Continuously analyzing the industry leaders and determining what they do better. A comparison against the best to provide targets for achievement.

Bottom line : Gross sales minus taxes, interest, depreciation, and other expenses. Also called net profit, net earnings, or net income.

Brainteaser : A type of case question in which the interviewee is asked to solve a riddle or logic problem.

Cannibalize : To take (sales) away from an existing product by selling a similar but new product usually from the same manufacturer; also: to affect (an existing product) adversely by cannibalizing sales.

Capital : Cash or goods used to generate income.

Case question : A fun, intriguing, and active interviewing tool used in consulting interviews to evaluate the multi-dimensional aspects of a candidate.

COGS : See costs of goods sold.

Core competencies : The areas in which a company excels.

Cost of goods sold (COGS) : On an income statement, the cost of purchasing raw materials and manufacturing finished products.

Cost-based pricing : A pricing strategy in which a product or service is priced according to the cost of producing, manufacturing, or otherwise creating the product or service. R&D and COGS are the major determinants in this pricing strategy.

Cost-benefit analysis : A technique designed to determine the feasibility of a project or plan by quantifying its costs and benefits.

Depreciation : A decrease in estimated value.

Distribution channel : Means by which a producer of goods or services reaches his or her final users.

Economy of scale : Reduction in cost per unit resulting from increased production, realized through operational efficiencies.

Fixed cost : A cost that does not vary depending on production or sales levels, such as rent, property tax, insurance, or interest expense.

Framework : A structure that helps you organize your thoughts and analyze a case in a logical manner.

Gross sales : Total value of sales, before deducting for customer discounts, allowances, or returns.

Growth phase : A phase of development in which a company experiences rapid earnings growth as it produces new products and expands market share.

Initial Public Offering (IPO) : The first sale of stock by a company to the public.

Interest expense : The money spent on the fee charged by a lender to a borrower for the use of borrowed money.

IPO : see Initial Public Offering.

Joint venture : An agreement between firms to work together on a project for mutual benefit.

Market share : The percentage of the total sales of a given type of product or service that are attributable to a given company.

Market-sizing question : A type of case question that is often called a back-of-the-envelope question. This type of question asks you to estimate the size of a specific market. An example: "How many pairs of boxer shorts are sold in the U.S. each year?"

Maturity phase : A phase of company development in which earnings continue to grow at the rate of the general economy.

Net sales : Gross sales minus returns, discounts, and allowances.

Niche market : A focused, targetable part of a market.

Overhead : The ongoing administrative expenses of a business, such as rent, utilities, and insurance.

Price-based costing : A pricing strategy in which a product or service is priced according to what the market will bear, or what the consumer is willing to pay.

Profit : The positive gain from a business or operation after subtracting for all expenses.

Proprietary : Something that is used, produced, or marketed under exclusive legal right of the inventor or maker; specifically: a drug (as a patent medicine) that is protected by secrecy, patent, or copyright against free competition as to name, product, composition, or process of manufacture.

R&D : see Research & Development.

Research & Development (R&D) : Discovering knowledge about products, processes, and services and then applying that knowledge to create new and improved products, processes, and services that fill market needs.

Revenue : Same as sales. The total dollar amount collected for goods and services provided.

Substitution : A product or service that fills a consumer's need in the same or similar way as another product or service (e.g., Nutrasweet is a substitution for sugar).

Supply and demand : The two key determinants of price. Supply is the total amount of a good or service available for purchase, while demand is the desire and ability by individuals to purchase economic goods or services at the market price.

Transition phase : A phase of development in which the company's earnings begin to mature and decelerate to the rate of growth of the economy as a whole.

Unit cost : Cost per item.

Variable cost : A unit cost which depends on total volume.

VC : see venture capital.

Venture capital (VC) : Funds made available for start-up firms and small businesses with exceptional growth potential. Managerial and technical expertise are often provided.

About the Author

Marc Cosentino is the Associate Director of Career Services at the John F. Kennedy School of Government at Harvard University. He is the former Assistant Director and Business Counselor at the Office of Career Services Harvard College. This is his third book on consulting.